Dear Michael Babara Kelsy & Tessa

Memories of your

African Safari

For Micheal a record

of some of the

pre "Getty Images"

Exploits of Messr Klein

& Getty — See Page 61

Great to have met

the Malone family.

Sincerely Dave

THE
Full
Circle

To Londolozi and Back Again
– A Family's Journey

DAVE VARTY

and Molly Buchanan

Penguin Books

PENGUIN BOOKS

Published By the Penguin Group
Penguin Books (South Africa) (Pty) Ltd, 24 Sturdee Avenue, Rosebank, Johannesburg 2196, South Africa
Penguin Books Ltd, 80 Strand, London WC2R 0RL, England
Penguin Group (USA) Inc, 375 Hudson Street, New York, New York 10014, USA
Penguin Group (Canada), 90 Eglinton Avenue East, Suite 700, Toronto, Ontario, M4P 2Y3, Canada (a division of Pearson Penguin Canada Inc.)
Penguin Ireland, 25 St Stephen's Green, Dublin 2, Ireland (a division of Penguin Books Ltd)
Penguin Group (Australia), 250 Camberwell Road, Camberwell, Victoria 3124, Australia (a division of Pearson Australia Group Pty Ltd)
Penguin Books India Pvt Ltd, 11 Community Centre, Panchsheel Park, New Delhi – 110 017, India
Penguin Group (NZ), 67 Apollo Drive, Mairangi Bay, Auckland 1310, New Zealand (a division of Pearson New Zealand Ltd)

Penguin Books (South Africa) (Pty) Ltd, Registered Offices:
24 Sturdee Avenue, Rosebank, Johannesburg 2196, South Africa

www.penguinbooks.co.za

First published by Penguin Books (South Africa) (Pty) Ltd 2008
Copyright text © David Varty 2008
Copyright photographs © David Varty 2008
The Times They are a-changin by Bob Dylan, reproduced courtesy of Special Rider Music
Copyright illustrations © Johan Hoekstra 2008

ISBN 9780143025764

Typeset in Palatino and Univers
Cover design and book design: mr design
Printed and bound by CTP Book Printers, Cape Town

In my many discussions with Dave, his friends and family, and in writing the story of his life I cannot help but think back on the words by Theodore Roosevelt, written nearly 100 years ago soon after his first visit to Africa:

'It is not the critic who counts: not the man who points out how the strong man stumbles or where the doer of deeds could have done better. The credit belongs to the man who is actually in the arena, whose face is marred by dust and sweat and blood, who strives valiantly, who errs and comes up short again and again, because there is no effort without error or shortcoming, but who knows the great enthusiasms, the great devotions, who spends himself for a worthy cause; who, at the best, knows, in the end, the triumph of high achievement, and who, at the worst, if he fails, at least he fails while daring greatly, so that his place shall never be with those cold and timid souls who knew neither victory nor defeat.'

Dave has faced many adversities in his life. His path has taken him out of his comfort zone and into the tough corporate world. But he has, nevertheless, recognised that without being drawn into that world, he would not have learnt the lessons that have given him the understanding and the weapons necessary to fight another day for conservation of this special continent. To go back to the words of Theodore Roosevelt, Dave has been willing to dare greatly. He has also succeeded greatly. For my part, I would like to see wind in his wings so that he will again soar.

Africa is a place of immense beauty. We need all the 'Dave's' of this world we can find to help keep this beauty intact.

Molly Buchanan

Molly Buchanan

I first met David Varty when he and Paul Bannister, the marketing director at CCAfrica, came to see me on a security-related matter in KwaZulu Natal. At the completion of our discussion, I asked their views of the recently launched South African world-wide marketing campaign. I was struck by the directness and forcefulness with which they both condemned the campaign. On the basis of their observations, I invited them to assist me with the restructuring of Satour on its way to becoming the SA Tourism Board. This gave me the opportunity to spend time with Dave Varty and it was inevitable that the conversation would turn to conservation and the key issue of the day – elephant culling.

Once again Dave was extremely forthright in his observations, suggesting that all conventional wisdom was outdated and that as minister I should extend the frontiers of land under wildlife, remove apartheid-invented security fences and expand the free range for elephants. A lively conversation ensued, which resulted in me accompanying Dave on a visit to Tanzania were I was impressed by the vast open systems of the Serengeti and Ngorongoro where people, cattle and wild life appeared to exist side by side in harmony, with little development and no fences.

Dave's passionate plea to drop fences which separated wildlife from wildlife in Southern Africa made a lasting impression on me and we worked together in taking the first steps in creating the Limpopo Transfrontier Park. His enthusiasm for river catchment protection led to my inspection of the head water catchment areas of rivers which feed into the Kruger National Park and are vital to the biodiversity of this wonderful asset. Flowing from this visit we were able to bring together many role players in the formation of the Blyde River Canyon Park.

This book is Dave's campfire story. It chronicles his relationship with Africa, her people and a variety of ambitious pioneering conservation development initiatives, and like all my conversations with Dave, the book is stimulating, controversial, intense and filled with a passion for the wellbeing of wildlife and the rural people of Africa.

Valli

Valli Moosa
Chairman, IUCN

D ave's book deserves much more than a foreword by me. Most of all, it needs to be read by as many people as possible. For that to be the case, it needs pithy quotes from publishers, journalists, critics and authors around the world. The sorts of things one sees on the covers and fly leaves of books in airports. Generally, these come with exclamation marks. 'A must-read!' springs to mind, as do 'exhilarating!', 'unputdownable!' and – my favourite – 'two thumbs up!' With these two thumbs up, Dave's life story will be able to make an even greater difference than Dave's life itself has.

I first met Dave in the early 1990s when he pitched up at Hambros Bank in London with his partner Alan Bernstein to convince us to help them raise money for the creation of a new game reserve and a new sustainable safari business model in KwaZulu Natal. For some inexplicable reason I was roped into the meeting. When Dave and Alan finished – which was many hours later – I told the Vice Chairman of the Bank, Christopher Sporborg, that I thought it was a bad idea. Christopher had made a career out of ignoring the advice of callow youths and now almost two decades later CCAfrica operates the largest safari business in the world. Its unique founding principles have ensured that the survival and growth of multiple species in the world's wild frontiers do not leave the local human communities behind. What Dave started has now become standard in the industry and has therefore shaped the debate about the tension between the animal kingdom and civilisation more than most. Dave and his brother, John, belong in a group of visionaries with David Attenborough, Jacques Cousteau, Dr Ian Player and Dian Fossey.

More than anything, Dave's book is a triumph of the spirit. Building CCAfrica was never easy. Never. Nor is it a completed story. It goes on. But it goes on without Dave. Like all revolutions, the energy required consumes the kindling you wish to burn as well as those closest to the flames. Burned and cast out, Dave's monument has been his ability to extract only good from all his experiences in life, even those that hurt him deeply.

I have learned whilst reading this book; I can only hope that many others will too. Two thumbs up!

Mark Getty

ACKNOWLEDGEMENTS

The Full Circle is, in many respects, a record of the many people I have encountered in my life who have crossed my path over the nearly 40 years since we founded Londolozi on our family farm in the bushveld lands of South Africa. I owe them all a huge debt of appreciation for the lessons that have flowed from them into my rich and varied life. Creating this manuscript has been a work in progress, principally drawing on the insights of these wonderful teachers, some of whom I acknowledge now, as having profoundly altered the course of my journey.

Firstly to my three fathers: Boyd Varty (snr), Harry Kirkman and Winnis Mathebula who ingrained in me a connection to this wild place called Londolozi. My amazing mother and mother of Londolozi and whose fortitude made it all possible. My life partner and twin flame Shan and mother to my wonderful children, Bronwyn and Boyd.

Dr Ken Tinley, a huge intellect and profound ecologist whose holistic approach was decades ahead of its time. Steuart Pennington and Enos Mabuza with their insights into the future and the importance of human dignity, mutual respect and continuous learning in the workplace.

The Londolozi family, rangers, trackers and staff, past, present and future who create the magic. Mark Getty, Allan Bernstein, Jonathan Klein and Christopher Sporborg who were my 'trackers' and 'guides' in the jungle of international corporate finance.

My partners at Londolozi for nearly four decades, John Varty and Allan Taylor who have overseen the birth of Londolozi, its close association with the rise of CCAfrica and Londolozi's rebirth in 2007 under family care.

My friend Paul Bannister an early reader of the manuscript, who gave constructive and at times somewhat harsh input on the pages as they unfolded, but who always made it clear that I should carry on and finish the story.

Finally to Molly Buchanan who has brought my voice through onto the pages of this book and has stayed the course. It would be entirely remiss of me if I were not to dwell on the herculean task and tireless inputs provided by Molly. In truth she has written the book twice. The first manuscript was described as a collection of anecdotal events but not a book. Molly worked to pare down the scattered collection of events and circumstances that were my life into a coherent story with a start a middle and an end – no mean task I might add. She has an indomitable spirit and her passion for writing has made an enormous contribution to the final result.

It has been my great pleasure to work with her and more recently with the Penguin publishing team headed by Alison Lowry, ably supported by Jane Ranger and Claire Heckrath, all of whom were introduced to us by Ron Irwin a literary agent in Cape Town. Shan and I have enjoyed working with this group of true professionals who have all made valuable contributions to shaping the books' final look and feel.

In conclusion, I wish to acknowledge the thousands of men and women across the world who are calling for greater reverence and respect for the natural world. Your collective voices are ushering in a new age of restoration and your momentum is requiring that the era of industrialisation and unbridled extraction from the natural world should now begin to yield to a new economic order one based on the laws of nature.

Dave Varty, June 2008

Dedicated to Shan, Bronwyn and Boyd, my unshakeable family

Sketch: Sue Deale

In writing the story of my life, I have tried to be accurate in my recollections of events as they affected other parties. But, in the end the views expressed are my personal ones and are not necessarily shared by others.

CONTENTS

Mission Statement

We aim to create a model
in wise land management
by using the many
qualities of the natural
system and by integrating
our visitors with
the environment and the
local people
to the benefit of all.

Our primary objective
is to demonstrate
that man and wildlife
can interact on
a sustainable basis.

Londolozi's mission statement – 1972 – still very applicable today

INTRODUCTION

Many people reading the stories in the pages of this book will simply not believe they're true. They really did happen; the tough times, the fun and laughter, the friends we made and the friends we lost. Along the way I learnt that what really counts in life is family and a handful of very dear friends. When you hit the headwinds, it is here that you ultimately find support.

I have been blessed with a wonderful wife and two dynamic, fun children and I could not have had kinder or more generous parents. I was only 15 when my father died but he left an indelible impression on me as a wonderful teacher. My mother was uncomplicated, wise and unconditionally loving. What more could we ask for? As I grew older I discovered that the values I learnt as a child are the ones that endure.

Our bushveld farm Sparta – which became Londolozi – had a profound effect on my early life. My first lessons were in hunting. We were brought up to track and shoot lions in the belief that the reduction of predators or 'vermin' would assist the rebuilding of game numbers which, in earlier times, had been decimated by the 'biltong hunters'. We shot impala, which were plentiful, but not those antelope which were scarce.

Then one day I knew that the killing was over. A new understanding permeated my being: nature's forces and wilderness restoration were a far greater challenge and a more rewarding option. I came to understand the implications of advancing green frontiers and just what it would take to attempt to turn back the politically motivated ideologies and flawed business principles that were leading to the destruction of the natural world. We would have to advocate for less of man's work in whatever was left untouched of the wilderness landscapes.

It became apparent to me – at the beginning of the new century – that South Africa had been blessed with a unique combination of human beings. Nelson Mandela, Walter Sisulu and their ANC associates inspired us with their strong bonds of camaraderie and – together with FW de Klerk – brought us the miracle of a new and vibrant South Africa. What a gift we have been given by these men: the rare qualities they shared with us and the heavy burden we have of honouring them and making our country work – no matter what.

The rough ride I have had in the last decade has triggered my own inner journey and this has been a special gift. It has taught me that things happen for a reason and within every perceived setback lies a new opportunity for inner growth. Through this personal story I hope that I may stimulate an inner awakening within the reader as to how we as individuals can play a part in extracting less from the planet as we go about our daily lives. Can we find a quality of life in the simpler things, no longer needing to consume ourselves to find happiness? Perhaps it is within each individual's consciousness that a solution to the long-term existence of our species resides.

What are our options? Can non-government organisations become a real force for change? Is it already happening? NGOs, making use of the Internet, have mounted successful global protests. But will governments and corporations heed the warnings? And can the most powerful force in the world – the economic machine – change its direction? Will an inner awakening, especially amongst individuals in future generations, cause a ripple of change that will develop with real purpose? Will money – currently the dominant force in this world – become an energy and a force for good? Do we place more importance on profit, growth and power rather than on care, love and compassion?

Living close to the wild African animals has taught me some things, particularly that though we may damage and destroy, nature will always have the last word. In time nature will override our mistakes. Life on this planet would be so much better if we understood that the workings of nature are more intelligent than we are and that haphazard interventions into this intelligent system have consequences that we can never truly anticipate. As Robert Green Ingersoll said a few hundred years ago: 'In nature there are neither rewards nor punishments. There are consequences.'

I sat with a dying man last week. He found it so valuable to hear the birds, to feel the breeze on his face, to see the light, and just to be. And most of all, to be connected to the energies that only nature can provide. This is all I could want for myself.

In the next stretch of my life, hopefully, I will embark on a journey from perceived success to real significance. What does this mean and where is it taking me? The pages in this book tell the story of my hopes.

More than anything, I have learnt that it is not the years of your life that count, it is the life in your years that really matter. In essence, it comes down to giving of your enthusiasm and of your best to each and every moment, before it passes you by.

John Kockelka 2000

We had worked right through the night. As I drove back to camp, all I could think of was getting my hands around a warm mug of coffee and then crawling into bed. But as the dawn broke I stopped to look around me. In the space of two months the landscape had changed. I could see across a mosaic of open grasslands and bushveld trees for perhaps a kilometre. And on lower ground a wetland vlei had filled with water which had not been there two days previously.

And then I noticed something different. Were my tired eyes playing tricks on me? Was it just the dappled light under the canopy of the tree? No, it was spots. I picked up my binoculars. And then I saw her. Not running away in fear. Not concerned at all. Just sitting and preening herself. She seemed oblivious to my presence. Then, she turned and looked directly at me and my heart stopped at her beauty and my fear that she would disappear and we would not see a leopard for another 10 years. Then she turned back to her task. But this time not to preen herself, but the two little cubs at her side.

I could hardly contain my excitement. We had been clearing the invasive bush for several months – for the previous six weeks we had worked night and day to make the most of a bulldozer that had been lent to us. At first little seemed to change. Then we noticed that grass was starting to grow again where we had taken out the trees. And now we had our vleis filling with water and a mother leopard had arrived from nowhere.

For us it was sheer magic. Or was it a gift from nature? It was one of the first lessons that I learnt in the bushveld. If you work with nature, she works with you in a forgiving and enduring partnership.

That first sighting of a leopard was a turning point in our lives. It marked the beginning of an upward spiral of success. Our safari business would become known all over the world because of the leopards of Londolozi. And we were on our way on a non-stop adventure.

THE SUDDEN AWAKENING

I entered the world of business by default soon after my father died. I was 15. My brother was three years older. We had as exciting a life as any boy could dream about growing up in South Africa in the 1960s. Cricket was my father's passion and, if we could, both John and I would have played the game, morning, noon and night. Every spare moment was spent with the cricket bat and ball – except for holidays which were spent at Sparta, the bushveld farm which my grandfather bought way back in 1926.

The hunting camp in what was then called the eastern Transvaal – only a few miles from the Kruger National Park – consisted of four small mud rondavels. It stayed virtually unchanged for half a century. My father was a strong but quiet man – except when he teased the life out of his friends and his family. He was born at a time when lions thrived on neighbouring cattle ranches and when conventional wisdom believed that reducing lion populations was a way to rebuild game numbers. Transvaal Consolidated Lands, which sold the land to my grandfather, reported to their shareholders in the early 1920s that the lions in the area had increased to more than 3 000. It was a somewhat questionable estimate, given that today that same area has about 120 lions. My guess is that it helped the directors explain why their cattle ranching activities were not successful. But there were many other reasons, the most significant being the poor soils and the fickle weather of the African subcontinent.

My brother and I had three 'fathers' as we grew up in the bushveld. Our own father was central to our early years: he grew up in an era in which lion hunting was a dangerous and thrilling adventure. But before his early death, he became aware that the wildlife of Africa would not survive unless it became a viable economic entity.

Then there was Harry Kirkman, one of the early game wardens who joined Colonel Stevenson-Hamilton and opened up the Kruger National Park on horseback. He was a man with a great love of the wild and an extraordinary judge

Wild days - Sparta hunting camp, circa 1940s

My three fathers.
Returning from a lion hunt with my father, Boyd Varty (top) Winnis
Mathebula (left) and Harry Kirkman (right)

of character. He was also reputed to have hunted and killed over a thousand lions. In his later years he became warden of the Sabi Sand Reserve where our family farm was situated. On many occasions as young boys, John and I would join him on anti-poaching patrols in the reserve.

Our third father was Winnis Mathebula who was born at the turn of the century and saw the true Africa when no roads or machines invaded its privacy. He witnessed the demise of a vast wild landscape in the face of exploding human populations and the arrival of the ghastly political ideologies of colonialism, fences and apartheid-based homeland systems which carved up this little piece of Africa. Winnis was a wonderfully entertaining raconteur and a naturalist who showed us how to gently harvest nature. He was our teacher, mentor and friend and a man of enormous wisdom and patience.

In truth, while Dad enjoyed the excitement of a lion hunt, most of all he loved the peace around the campfire and the simplicity of bushveld life. He wanted the place to stay wild. Perhaps, too, he liked to get away from social trivialities for which he had little patience. His great friend Tom Robson once complained: 'Varty, why don't you fix the bloody road to your camp?' His reply was to the point: 'If I fixed it, silly arses like you would come and visit me too often!' And they would laugh their heads off and have another beer around the campfire.

Dad only ever allowed two tracks on the entire property and when it rained, everyone got stuck. He would tell us that beyond the river that ran through our property, 'You buggers must walk.' We did not know it then, but he was way ahead of his time in recognising that those last wild lands would slowly become overrun with tracks as more and more people visited the bushveld.

Dad wanted his sons to grow up quickly. There was a reason for this. He had suffered from rheumatic fever when he was young and did not have a strong heart. Nevertheless, he was one of the four per cent who made it back after flying twice over Warsaw to drop supplies for the Polish resistance in the last months of the Second World War. The return flight of the defenceless SAAF 31 Squadron Liberators, which flew over several countries in hostile hands as well as part of Germany, took 10 hours and 40 minutes. Their limit of fuel endurance was 11 hours. It took men of great courage to fly those missions and it was not surprising that Dad believed that boys became men either through wartime flying or hunting lions. His ambition was to live long enough to see each of his sons shoot a lion and in his eyes become a man. It was his belief that facing death and conquering fear were essential elements in preparing his boys for the world beyond schooldays and cricket.

He loved children and he taught me and John to hunt, instilling discipline and independence at an early age. I was only six when Dad gave me the hunting rifles to clean. He also gave us a lot of his time and taught us well. Then he left us to get on with the job. To this day I can recall the weapons he placed in my care and the lessons he gave me: how to assemble a Webley Scott shotgun with interchangeable barrels, the Mauser action on the four 30.06 rifles, all of which had been home-built, the way to identify the bolts for the different rifles, and my dad's pride and joy – the Rigby 416, the only weapon he ever bought over the counter. It replaced the home-built 404 that fed two bullets at once and nearly got him eaten by a lion one eventful morning when the gun jammed. My mother recorded the story in the Sparta game book which she kept until my father died. She wrote, 'Boyd had a narrow shave today. But, as usual, he kept his head. Surrounded by lions and with a gun that had jammed, he hoisted his guest into a tree and then stood shoulder to shoulder with Winnis Mathebula glaring at the lions. The lions continued to threaten the two but after a while they retreated.'

Dad gave me my first taste of trust and independence. It never crossed his mind that once he had finished teaching us we would do something stupid. He did not dominate us, his whole approach to our upbringing was simply to give us the opportunity to succeed or learn from our mistakes. If food needed to be cooked he would say, 'Cook the food yourself.' If the Land Rover broke down, he would say, 'Make a plan.' If we got a puncture, he would say, 'Fix the damned thing.' If you wounded an impala, he would say, 'Don't come back until you've got it.' If you said you'd nearly been bitten by a snake, he'd ask, 'What kind of snake?' It was an endless lesson in independence, a privilege that few kids are given today. There'd be little sympathy but a lot of love, fun and teasing. It was a great foundation for our lives. Hunting was Dad's means of teaching us discipline, independence and trust.

In truth, I was always a lousy hunter. My first impala took me 11 shots. I remember the occasion as if it was yesterday. It was July 1962

and I was eight years old. There was a drought and it was very cold.
The earth looked like a clay tennis court and in the early winter dawn
the bare trees looked like ghosts. I took my 30.06, which Dad had fitted
with a muzzle-breaker to reduce the recoil and a shortened stock to fit
my young shoulders. It was almost too heavy for me to lift. The impala,
with his body facing away from me, had turned his head towards me.
I fired and missed the impala's neck where I was aiming but hit it
straight up the arse. The bullet broke the animal's spine, anchoring it
to the ground. Nonetheless, it looked very big and dangerous to an
eight-year-old as it thrashed around in a futile attempt to escape. At
about 20 yards I fired off four more bullets, missing every time. The
tears were streaming down my face and I was breathing heavily. My
father stood by and watched.

'Get closer,' he instructed. 'Finish it off.'

'I've no more bullets Dad.'

'That's a big mistake. Go! Get them! And make it quick.'

My hands were shaking so badly that half the bullets dropped into
the sand but I managed to reload the gun with five more bullets. He
could see I was terrified but continued to look on. Then he took me in
closer. Wham! Wham! Wham! Another five bullets missed and I had to
reload a second time before, at point blank range, I eventually put the
poor animal out of its misery. That day he taught me that if you start
something, you have to finish it. It was a lesson etched in my brain for
a lifetime. I learnt that if the impala had been a lion, I would have been
eaten and that one should always prepare for any eventuality because
things can go wrong.

Four years later Dad decided I was old enough to take on a lion.
Picture the scene: I woke up before dawn, freezing cold, a mug of hot
coffee warming my hands while I listened. And then we heard a roar
right next to the camp. There would be no escape.

'Oh my God!' I thought. 'Is this really happening?'

The three of us took off. Dad and Winnis Mathebula, our guardian
and expert lion tracker, both ready for action. And trembling me. It
was dark as we walked down the road in the direction of the lion. It
roared so loudly that my teeth rattled. I wished like crazy that the lion
would go away, but at the same time I wanted to please my father.
Then we stopped. The lion was too close and we would meet up with
him before dawn broke. It would still be too dark to take the shot.

St...

Visitors :   McDonald - Towlon
Mr Kerring - Trennie.
Fielden Kariro. Mr L...
Barberton

Species Seen: Impala. wildebeo...   ...buck
baboon, zebra, ...
stembuck, cala,
snake. tortoise

Species Shot :
Impala   Rupert with Picann.. } Pad-eye Pi...

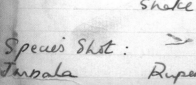

Haig was a hunter - - - -

Came from Graaff - Reinet - - - - -

John - last camp
to

Winnis and Dad conferred in urgent whispers: Do we go back? Should we sit and wait? Or do we move forward? We decided to sit. The seconds dragged by in absolute silence as we waited for the next roar. Then the dawn broke and the lion roared again. I felt that he was right on top of us. But Winnis detected that the direction of the roar had changed slightly and we had to move forward quickly or lose the opportunity. The first light was coming through the trees as we crept into position. Could we see our sights? Yes. And then, around a tree directly ahead of us on the game path, a huge dark shape was coming towards me.

'That's it. Make the shot,' Dad said quietly.

I positioned myself as I had been taught. I could see the lion clearly. It was light enough for me to line him up in my sights. I had run out of excuses. The lion lifted its head for an instant and I was presented with a full frontal chest shot 60 yards away. But my breathing was out of control. It wasn't just my hands that were shaking, my whole body was beyond receiving messages from my brain. It was a freezing July dawn and I was bathed in sweat. My hesitation cost me the shot. The lion bolted.

Dad did not reprimand me. He did not even show his disappointment. His lesson was, you don't take a shot unless you are confident of a clean kill. Those were the rules he taught and the ones he lived by. As a teacher he was always consistent. You always knew where you stood because he stuck to what he taught – no matter what. Even his disappointment made no difference. It was three more years before that lion hunt was completed.

In 1968, one year before he died, Dad was charged by a rogue elephant. In 1926, when the Kruger Park was proclaimed, there were no elephants. They had bolted into the swamps of Mozambique where they would be safe from the ivory hunters. When the sounds of gunfire died down, they returned to the Kruger slowly and, after the fence between the Kruger and the Sabi Sand was put up in the 1960s, there were only a few on our side of the Sand River. The result was that Dad and Winnis had little experience of elephants.

One morning they were out on a walk – not on a hunt at all – when they came upon a single bull elephant. Dad was carrying a light calibre rifle, a 30.06. The elephant charged and Dad fired all five shots before he turned the animal at seven paces but he did not kill it. It was a close call for Dad and Winnis. Neither really understood elephants but the rules which applied to all wounded animals had to be followed. It was the last day of our July holiday but Dad cancelled his return to Johannesburg and all the business meetings that had been lined up, and said that he and Winnis were going after the elephant.

He got permission from the warden of the Kruger Park where the elephant had headed, and they tracked the wounded animal on foot for five days. Such was the importance to my Dad of the ethics of hunting. He taught us that a wounded animal was to be tracked and finished off at all costs. Eventually the KNP officials helped him. When they found and destroyed the elephant they discovered that it had a muzzle-loaded musket slug in its tusk and three other old musket wounds in its head. Small wonder that the elephant charged men on sight.

On another occasion my Dad and Winnis went into tough riverine bush looking for a leopard that might have been wounded. Then one of the party cleared his throat. The next second he was staring into the barrels of four guns. My father was furious and let his guest know it without mincing his words. He and Winnis would have rather tracked 10 wounded lions than one wounded leopard. A lion growls and then goes for you. Leopards are silent hunters. They only growl after they have their claws around the neck of their victim.

Soon after my fifteenth birthday, Dad went off with his hunting mates on a guineafowl shoot to the Ellisras area in the Limpopo, leaving me and my cousin Ian Thomas at Sparta. He planned to return about 10 days later to collect us and did not give a second thought to leaving two kids on their own in the bush with hunting rifles, booze and vehicles. He was confident in our training and believed that we could handle whatever situation arose. As insurance, Winnis Mathebula was there to make sure we did not get into any scrapes.

When Harry Kirkman arrived unexpectedly at the camp, bringing me the news that my father's heart had given up while on the guineafowl shoot, it was like the end of the world for me. The central figure of my life – the hunter, the teacher, our cricket coach – was gone. He had brought laughter and excitement into our lives and taught us to care and to love. I was 15 years old. My brother was spending the year doing compulsory military service in the South African Air Force and I felt alone and devastated. Even now, 38 years later, his death on 30 August 1969 remains a deeply emotional moment in my life.

The pioneers - the Varty and Unger families setting up camp, 1928

My father's death put the family in a precarious financial position and there were huge decisions that had to be made. At the centre of this drama stood Maidie Varty, my mother and mother of Londolozi. She was a widow with three children waiting to complete schooling and university. My father's business was leaderless and vulnerable. Added to that, soon after my father died in 1969, the stock market crashed and she had to find the money to pay estate duties calculated on a much higher valuation than became the reality.

There was no doubt that the easy way out for her was to sell our beloved Sparta. For two years its future hung in the balance while the advisers assessed the options open to her. They had no doubt that her best decision would be to sell the farm. I remember one of her advisers telling her that if she sold Sparta she could be assured of an income of R76 000 a year. I intervened, and with my 16 years of accumulated wisdom told them that I would earn my mother R76 000 a month! The retort was, 'Young man, you've got a big mouth. I certainly hope you can back the way you speak!'

John and I were vociferous in pleading to keep the farm, not under-standing for one minute what that meant, how much it would cost and what the implications for my mother would be. But, despite the uncertainty and the singular lack of a plan from her two teenage sons, she chose not to sell and followed the far more difficult route for herself. In an extraordinary selfless gesture, she gave John and me the opportunity to use the farm, provided we could cover the costs ourselves.

John and I felt under an obligation to our father to get university degrees. Our mother helped us, paying our fees to complete our education. Beyond this she had no capital for a fledgling safari busi-ness. John completed his military service the year my father died while I postponed mine until after I finished university. The result was that we were first-year university students together.

The night before our first year business administration exams, John pulled the word 'Londolozi' ('the protector of all living things') out of a Zulu dictionary and our safari business was born. We had no doubt that this was where our future lay.

From the beginning, our R3-a-day safari business was a disaster

WHERE ANGELS FEAR TO TREAD – 1970

From the beginning, our R3-a-day safari business was a disaster. Londolozi's assets consisted of four mud huts, a team of Shangaan men including Winnis Mathebula, our master lion tracker now turned guide, Two-Tone Sithole who knew all about tracking and lion hunting but nothing about the hospitality business, and Spook Sithole – our resident cook. It was hand-to-mouth stuff. But we got by because Dad had given us the foundation for our lives. He gave us a deep love for family, for land, for the bush and the wildlife, and a practical training in hunting which became the basis of our photographic safaris.

As well as our ability to find animals, what carried us forward was the human dynamic. Everyone was passionate about what they were doing. And we were breaking new ground. Hunting had given way to photographic safaris and we learnt that interpreting wildlife is an enriching experience. Hunting gave us invaluable knowledge of tracking dangerous animals but studying the birds, insects, reptiles and frogs opened a new dimension of understanding for us.

Until I finished university I joined John over weekends whenever I could. During this time, a young girl with 'Wednesday legs' (When's dey gonna break?) came into my life. Her name was Shan Watson. She was still at school and, at 15, still wearing bobby socks and a panama hat, but with all the potential of long-legged beauty. I certainly noticed her and a few months later when I was short of a date, I phoned her. All I talked about was our bushveld farm called Sparta. I wanted her to see the land and the animals and share my dream. Her parents eventually caved in under the relentless pressure from my 17-year-old self with no driver's licence, no money and some crazy idea about building a safari camp in some remote part of South Africa. They gave us permission to go to the farm for the weekend but said that her big sister had to accompany her to keep her safe. This was no problem. I quickly organised a big ranger to distract the big sister and the rest – as they say – is history. I was on my way on a beautiful journey through life with a friend and companion who would in time become my wife, the mother of my children, a business colleague and my soulmate.

There was also a growing group of student friends. Howard Mackie, 'the good companion', was one of the first to join us. Others soon followed and many laid the foundations for their future careers: David Lawrence became deputy chairman of Investec Bank, Mike Myers has become a renowned guide with Wilderness Safaris, Ken Maggs became head of security and game capture at South African National Parks, Map Ives has become the world authority on the Okavango Delta, Liz Westby-Nunn became the founder of the Portfolio of Places, Lex Hes operates and owns the very successful Ecologics game ranger training centre and Chris Badger heads up Wilderness Safaris Malawi. My cousin Ian Thomas used his observations on lions for the groundwork of his first motivational presentation, *The Power of the Pride*, which he subsequently published. The ideas that he developed in those early years paved the way for a hugely successful international career as a motivational speaker.

Ian and I grew up together. I even jumped a year at school – going from kindergarten straight into Grade 2 – to be in the same class with him. From then on we went through school playing cricket and rugby together and getting crapped on by our fathers every time our school reports arrived. But we each had one saving grace. Ian was the fastest bowler in the school. And I did my bit with the bat. So, although we were always in trouble about our school marks, because our fathers loved sport, we managed to survive their wrath.

As kids we hunted lions together but when Ian joined us as a ranger at Londolozi I watched as he grew to love all aspects of the wilderness. He loved lions. He especially loved tracking lions, studying lions, photographing lions. And when our most notorious male lion, Big Black, who put hearts into the mouths of visitors and rangers alike, was shot on a neighbouring farm, Ian went into mourning. He even gave me his resignation. He felt there was no point in going into the bush without Big Black there to growl at him.

As young men we shared a common vision and passion and we worked hard. Lex Hes spent every moment he could walking the property gathering knowledge and data about the birds, animals, plants and insects

I was on my way on a beautiful journey through life with a friend and companion who would in time become my wife, the mother of my children, a business colleague and my soulmate, August 1980.

We were a bunch of kids of the 70s: long-haired, bearded, scruffy, careless with time and clothing.

– information that now forms the basis of a curriculum for any aspirant game ranger. Lex did not need any motivation or direction. He had a passion for what he was doing. Howard Mackie could fix almost anything. He frequently worked through the night so that the old Land Rover would be ready for our guests at dawn – after we had borrowed a drum of fuel from Mala Mala. We'd pay for the fuel with the cash received from the guests who had just left.

We were a group of like-minded young people, most of us not even out of our teens. But we had all the answers to all the questions. We were bulletproof and brimful of confidence. The world was waiting for us and we were scared of nothing. There was no doubt in our minds that we would run the best safari operation in the world. We were a bunch of kids of the 70s: long-haired, bearded, scruffy, careless with time and clothing. But we were dedicated to giving our guests a thrilling adventure, and even if it was pretty terrifying for a guest to face a pride of lions on foot with only a bunch of long-haired kids wielding guns to protect them, we knew our business. Dad's training was indelibly imprinted on our minds.

While our ability to find lions became renowned, we did not have the first idea about hospitality. We asked guests to bring their own food and drink. Then, as part of the service, we'd offer them back their own beer and swap their supermarket specials for our rather tough impala cooked by Spook Sithole, Londolozi's chef extraordinaire. Spook knew how to cook impala: impala roast, impala steak, impala brains, impala stew, impala livers, impala biltong. You had a serious problem if you were not partial to impala, particularly if you were staying at Londolozi for weeks on end. Eventually we realised we had to change our catering system when we found we had hundreds of rancid margarine blocks piling up in our 'pantry' which was simply a mud hut where the rats and snakes thrived.

What was magical was that we were one big family and when guests stepped into Londolozi, they became part of that family. We had a common goal and an energy that was supercharged. We tried anything. It was within this spirit of independence that our management techniques were instinctively born. They differentiated Londolozi from many others in the hospitality industry. Londolozi was never created to fit into a professional hotel-type mould. Adventure, game viewing and entertainment came first. The things that drove Londolozi were raw

enthusiasm, like-mindedness, clear leadership, a strong culture, self-guidance towards common objectives, a strong group consciousness, aligned interests, harmony and caring – things that large, modern-day organisations can only dream about.

If our one and only Land Rover broke down – as it frequently did – we took guests on walking safaris. Once our Land Rover caught fire, sending guests scattering in all directions. But, within hours, we managed to get it going again. On another occasion, the gear stick snapped while in reverse and John had to drive back to camp in reverse with guests lighting matches to show the way. Or the Land Rover would break down miles from anywhere. We had no radio communication. But soon we had a bush party going and hours after we failed to return, a search party would find us singing around a fire in some remote part of the property. Our unreliable transport eventually became impossible and we were lucky to persuade our grandmother to lend us R500 to buy a second-hand Land Rover and double the size of our fleet.

On one occasion John, Winnis and I came upon a pride of lions that had just killed a wildebeest. Winnis had spent a lifetime as a hunter/gatherer and meat was the biggest delicacy in his life – especially after hunting by the indigenous people was outlawed as poaching. Winnis could not stand by and watch the lions eating all that beautiful meat. It was too much of a temptation for him. He had a singular contempt for lions and gave us kids the plan. He would walk in and take the meat from the 'inja' – the dogs. We were to bring in the Land Rover so that we could hack the meat into pieces and load the vehicle while he kept the lions at bay. But the plan went wrong. When we were about to take off we discovered that, with the additional weight of the wildebeest meat, the vehicle had sunk deep into the mud. We would have to get out, unload and dig the Land Rover out with lions all around us. They were hungry and irritable but this did not concern Winnis at all. One of the first things he had done was to cut off the wildebeest tail as a gift for his wife who was a herbalist sangoma and for whom he had far more respect than for any lion. Winnis swished the wildebeest tail in the lions' faces while we threw pieces of meat back to them. Eventually nothing much was left and we

A final salute - the passing of a Land Rover, which broke in half.
Wife of Winnis Mathebula - we risked life and limb for a wildebeest tail.

had no choice but to beat a nervous retreat back to camp on foot. All the comment we got from Winnis was, 'Aah! Dammit!'

So we had four mud huts and two dilapidated Land Rovers, and a wonderful team of enthusiastic young people but no hoteliers. But that didn't stop us from going ahead and advertising: accommodation for 10. It sounded like a nice round number and we never gave the logistics of fitting 10 people into four huts a thought. Did we plan to put three people in a room – or four? I don't think we planned at all. On top of that we had no electricity, no running water, let alone hot water, and no flushing toilets. The beds were farm gates with welded pipes as legs and coir mattresses that pricked. There was no bed linen. Instead we had army issue blankets which you wound around yourself when you went to bed.

When guests arrived at the weekend we all moved out of the huts and into the prefab storeroom which we had salvaged from our father's office in Johannesburg. There would be one long party – and more often than not the guests would join us. After the party 10 or more of us would be sleeping on the floor. It was communal living to the full. The last man to wake next morning would often find no khaki clothes to wear and would go to work in the pyjamas of the guy who had just left – if he was lucky enough to find them!

The first brochure we ever brought out advertised luxury safaris, rough safaris, wilderness walking, and canoe safaris. Yes. Using our slender resources we planned instantly to dominate all sectors of the safari industry. The fact that we could not paddle a canoe more than a hundred yards on the Sand River did not deter us. We went ahead and bought five inflatable canoes. On a perfect day on our river, a party of five rangers and visitors set off from the big granite rocks in front of our camp. They went about 50 metres and then, around the first bend, they came face to face with a hippo in the middle of the pool. Because there was so little water, there was not enough room for the boats and the hippo. One of our guests left his canoe by grabbing an overhead branch and swinging, monkey-style, into a tree. His canoe swept past the hippo which dived for cover and disappeared. The rest of the party abandoned ship. This marked the end of what was our one and only day in the canoe safari business.

Game drives were not that much better. I recall one eventful outing with our trusty Land Rover loaded to the gills with 10 guests, our tracker and me. A 1959 Series II Land Rover does not cope well with such a load in rugged driving conditions. I found myself lying under the Land Rover staring at a collapsed front suspension and a steering mechanism that had parted company with the steering wheel. This Land Rover was not going anywhere for several days. Undaunted, I leapt back to my feet and told the expectant guests that a walk was perhaps a good option for the afternoon's adventure.

One of our first groups of guests was an overflow from Mala Mala. They arrived unexpectedly at about five o'clock in the evening. I asked Two-Tone, 'Basisa yindlu,' clean the room. He had never done housework, but he realised there was a crisis, so he climbed onto the bed – wearing his tractor-tyre open sandals – and began to sweep the dust and the insects off the mattress. Clouds of dust billowed in all directions. Our French guests peered over my shoulder into the room. Their eyes were like saucers. We had to make a hasty exit before we were asphyxiated.

There was no electricity. Instead there was the friendly glow of paraffin lanterns and the open fire which was lit at dusk as it had been in the routine of camp life for the past 50 years. Soon the fire started to crackle and Spook put a leg of impala on the fire to feed our sophisticated party of French men and women. Out came the enamel mugs, the tin plates and the cutlery reminiscent of a bygone era, all clean but showing signs of their years of hard wear. It probably was as well that we did not understand what the French guests were saying. But their feelings were clear. They left the next morning before breakfast.

The next party was, if anything, worse. A group of my mother's friends, horror of all horrors, booked the 'luxury safari'. The idea was that guests would arrive by private charter at the Mala Mala runway which we had been given permission to use. After a pleasant day of game viewing, they would be flown to a nearby luxury hotel for the night (only a few minutes flying time away). The next morning they would return for another day in the bush, ending with a scenic bush dinner. Without any radio communication it turned out to be a logistical nightmare when appalling weather played havoc with our carefully laid plans. This was our baptism by fire into the safari industry.

As dawn broke on our first great African luxury safari we were ready. But not for the weather. It rained in biblical proportions. Even Noah would have been impressed. The planes should never have landed on the waterlogged runway, but they did. There was so much water that they came in looking more like motor boats.

Londolozi
canoeing

Guests participating in the "LONDOLOZI SAFARI" can make arrangements to canoe two mile section of the Sand River. This is subject to river conditions and guests will be made full- aware of the risks involved.

There will be an extra charge of R5 per person for such a canoe trip.

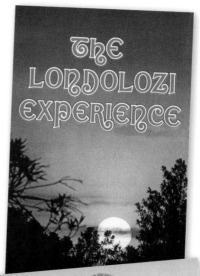

THE LONDOLOZI EXPERIENCE

LONDOLOZI
GAME RESERVE

Londolozi turns back the clock...
See the Africa of old...unspoilt today.

Londolozi is situated in the heart of the biggest private game reserve in the world. It's totally unspoilt, unexplored and just as raw as the Africa of old. Londolozi (which means protector of living things) provides an excellent opportunity to view and photograph both big and small game, from open landrovers accompanied by a game ranger

Wild life enthusiasts, whether they be tourists or businessmen, can now avoid the usual overcrowded game park atmosphere. Londolozi admits only 10 people at any one time. Your stay is thus unique, personal and offers the maximum opportunity to see the animals in their natural environment.

Man

LONDOLOZI
GAME RESERVE

A Diary of the Londolozi Experience

| *Evolution of the Londolozi marketing brochures dating back to 1972*

Our guests got off the planes ashen-faced after a very bumpy ride and climbed into the open air Land Rovers in pouring rain – not a good start.

The first game drive was appalling. No animals. Not even an impala. Just water, mud and long wet grass everywhere. We tried hard to give them an exciting experience but failed abysmally. Instead we got stuck in the mud and eventually arrived back at the airstrip rather late. Somehow or other the two planes got airborne for their short flight to the hotel. One plane landed near the hotel where they were staying – but on the wrong runway. The pilot managed to pull up just 20 metres short of the trees and, for the second time that day, the ashen-faced guests climbed out of the plane. But there was no one to meet them and they stood miserably waiting in the pouring rain. Eventually the driver of the combi we had hired to transfer the guests to the hotel made his way over to them and with relief they headed for luxury and comfort.

In the meantime the pilot of the first plane radioed through to the second plane: 'Don't land here. The runway's too short,' he told them. So plane number two turned back to the Mala Mala airstrip and was faced with a virtual night landing onto a wet bush strip. We 'safari heroes' had settled down at Londolozi to discuss the events of the day when a plane flew overhead in the direction of the Mala Mala runway. Realising that something must have gone wrong, we tore back only to find once again a bedraggled group of visitors standing next to the plane which had performed a miraculous landing in the fading light. Now what? Half the party was in the comfortable luxury hotel. Or so we thought. The other half were still in the bush and it was still raining. It was too late to fly so we bundled them aboard our rickety, non-roadworthy and unlicensed open Land Rover and drove them for two hours in the pouring rain to their hotel. They got there cold, wet and miserable. Day one of Londolozi's luxury safari was over!

It says something for their staying power that they returned the next day to complete their safari which was rounded off with a grand finale bush banquet. At least it had stopped raining. But stinkbugs had emerged in their millions. The menu went like this: impala steaks and stinkbugs, beans and mixed vegetables with stinkbugs. Tapioca pudding topped with – you guessed it – stinkbugs! If you have ever had the misfortune to accidentally swallow a stinkbug, believe me, it is an experience you would not wish to repeat. Coffee, tea and chocolates were abandoned as the guests were overrun with stinkbugs. They departed on their two-hour road transfer back to their hotel never to return again. Needless to say, my mother insisted that we refund their money. Perhaps this safari was a message to us: the safari business is definitely not for sissies.

When Gordon Dunningham and the Royston families first arrived from the wealthy northern suburbs of Johannesburg, the Londolozi farm was really rough. It was the Easter weekend in early April and the grass was so tall in the middle of the track that you could hardly see where you were going. Waiting to greet them at the four mud huts on the bank of the Sand River was the same scruffy mob of youngsters wielding 30.06 guns. The mud huts were small, only five metres in diameter. There were no flushing toilets, only a long-drop 60 yards away, canvas basins with water to wash in and a hose strung over a branch to shower under. Whether you liked it or not, there was cold water summer and winter – except for a few brief moments when you enjoyed the warm water that had been in the section of pipe exposed to the sun. Water was always a big issue. Things were always going wrong. We sometimes had boiling water in the toilets: when we ran out of water, the hot water from the donkey boilers would go backwards down the cold-water plastic pipes, giving guests a remarkable experience of sitting on a steaming toilet before the whole thing would burst and we'd have no water at all.

Catering presented an equally difficult situation: our make-shift cool box (a wet cloth hung over a wire cage) was not all that effective on a hot day. After the entire party came down with a serious bout of diarrhoea, Gordon Dunningham was heard to comment, 'These guys will be out of business before the end of the month!' That was it: the Land Rover was buggered, it was raining and the roofs were leaking, there was nowhere to eat, the food went off and everyone was wet. To top it all, I got lost and the Land Rover broke down and several of the party got tick bite fever.

It seems an unlikely end to the tale but they all came back and became great friends – despite the accommodation and despite the food. But they brought their pills with them just in case they had bad food again. What we learnt was that human interface was the most important aspect of any safari. To this day we remember the families at Londolozi: one of our roads is named the Royston Road in acknowledgement of the worst safari ever given.

But slowly things began to improve. We put planks across the Land Rover for people to sit facing forwards instead of sideways. This was far more comfortable when we added a bit of sponge on the seat – which Two-Tone Sithole tied to the plank with a bit of rubber from an old inner tyre tube. We got the sponge offcuts cheaply. There was no backing to the seats. Then the planks were removed and we went upmarket with drop-in seats which had backrests. This was design par excellence as we could remove the seats between game drives to load rubbish, the firewood or the dead impala, and then wash out the vehicle and put the seats back ready for the next game drive. Sometimes, when we hadn't done our job properly, we'd be followed by a strange, unpleasant aroma and, understandably, our guests would complain.

When we were selected by Barlows as a getaway experience for their executives, we were given an advance payment to help us prepare the new wilderness trails camp for their visit. Our priorities were tents and a beautiful shiny water tank so that our guests would have a reliable water supply at their campsite. It took longer than we anticipated to build the four-metre stand for the tank, but it was unquestionably an engineering masterpiece – or so we thought. Unfortunately we ran late and were only able to start filling the tank the morning the guests were due to arrive. At least the pump worked and the water flowed strongly into the tank. All was well.

As we watched the tank fill, from the other direction we could hear the guest cars arriving. We stood back to admire our handiwork. This time we were confident that we were well prepared for the safari. At that moment I saw the three-quarters full tank start to move. The stand with the water tank on top, which we had built at a cost of more than six months' turnover, was buckling under the weight of the water. It hit the deck at the same moment our guests arrived. This would be another weekend without water and there would have to be some explaining from our side. One thing was certain, there was no danger of any of us ever becoming engineers. Fortunately our guests were very forgiving. If there was no running water in camp, they could wash in the river. It was insignificant alongside the thrilling experience we were able to lay on for them.

When Ross Parry-Davies (chairman of the geotechnical division of LTA) arrived as a guest, I took him for a walk because the Land Rover had once again broken down. But when we stopped for a rest, I fell asleep. We had worked the whole night trying to repair the vehicle.

He said to me, 'You look like rather a worn-out young man. What's up?'

So I told him about our problems. How our top priority was to have flushing toilets. He helped me design an ablution block and taught me a whole raft of things about plumbing. Nipples, sockets, pipethreaders, unions, joints all were terms new to me. That December he arrived with plumbing materials salvaged from a hotel in Johannesburg that was about to be demolished. That was how we got our first bathroom facilities. They still stand at the Londolozi Camp – even though every year management wants to knock them down. We resist, telling them that for us it is like asking permission to knock down the Sistine Chapel.

We built a tree house for guests so they could sleep out for the night. Winnis, Two-Tone and Spook requested a meeting. Why, they asked, when we had four lovely huts, did we take our guests to sleep in a tree? They did not understand. Nor did they understand why we tracked lions, found them and no longer shot them. That really was a puzzle.

Notwithstanding all our debacles, somewhere along the line the Johannesburg and Durban mink-and-manure crowd started to find out about us: a wild bunch of youngsters in a great wildlife area with an uncanny ability to track lions and all at a cost of R3 a day. When guests arrived – often in the middle of the night – we would welcome them to the fire, the beers would be opened and it would be the start of a wild weekend. We would party all night, walk up to lions at dawn, sometimes go on game drives, party on the river and hardly sleep at all.

Guests began arriving, first in small numbers for weekend breaks. And then the Johannesburg crowd started to come in a continuous stream and Londolozi was on its way to becoming a well-known adventure destination.

Sometimes the weekend would end with a game of soccer in the car park, which we gave up because too many hamstrings were torn. Then we would play leggie (a competitive game in which each team would try to get the ball through the opponent's legs) before our exhausted guests would depart, nursing their sand-burns, cuts and scratches and, more often than not, their sore heads!

Of course, on their return home, our guests would brag that it was costing them far less than the price charged by our more famous neighbours, to see the same lion. It was all done in fun but did not assist with neighbourly relations.

From dawn to dusk and in-between - safari is a 24/7 business.
Bushveld soccer, described by a guest as a substitute for tribal warfare.

Added to that, the lovely girls working 'next door' started to take pity on us and would arrive with leftover food from their kitchen, all on plates and mugs bearing our neighbour's crest. Eventually it had to stop. One eventful day the manager of Mala Mala arrived to discuss a problem. We invited him to join us for dinner but we were one tin plate short. Spook picked out the only smart china plate which he gave our guest. But when the manager started to clear his plate of peas and potatoes, he discovered the Mala Mala crest. 'What's this?' he asked us. Fortunately he thought it was a great joke that we had served him dinner on his own crockery.

We also had another problem. At the outset, we realised that if we wanted a viable safari business, we needed more land. But, when we asked our neighbour Tom Robson if we could have traversing rights over his property as we were giving up university and going into our Londolozi business full-time, he refused. Tom had promised our father, his great friend, that he would ensure that we finished university. 'First get your degrees,' Tom said. 'And then we'll talk about it.' So we spent several more years, John and I sharing the load of studying and running our business. I did everything I could for John at the Johannesburg end – everything except write his final exams – which gave John more time to look after the farm and the guests.

Slowly, things were coming together. And despite our inexperience, we even found the time to formulate opinions on conservation and pretty much any other subject in the universe. At a wildlife conference in the early 1970s we delivered a paper on the economic viability of wildlife. We thought we had all the answers. We were called wildlife mercenaries. The National Parks Board officials told us we were a disgrace. We were labelled impostors in the conservation world. Comments like, 'I will not sit here and listen to Mr Varty telling us how we should be making money out of wildlife', and, 'Open Land Rovers are a gimmick that should not be permitted in any game reserve', got John on a roll. 'If I can eat it, if I can hunt it, if I can photograph it, that is what I will do. I will make money out of wildlife!'

We were thrown out of the conference and thrown out of the offices of nature conservation in the Kruger National Park. Our thinking was too radical for the times. But we took that route because we had no choice if we were to pay the bills.

What we did not know then was that our road would eventually influence the African National Congress and South Africa's new government would follow more enlightened and progressive conservation and water policies. And that before the end of the millennium, the National Parks would be faced with the same predicament. Eventually they, too, would have no choice. They would follow us in being forced to find ways to make wildlife pay.

In 1976 I 'retired' from a promising cricket career. Our team had just won the Johannesburg premier league – one of the most competitive and high standard cricket leagues in the country. It was unheard of for a promising young player to give up the game at 21. But the reality was that South Africa was no longer in the international arena and my dream of playing international cricket had died. Many will recall the Basil D'Oliveira affair of 1968/69, when prime minister John Vorster refused to allow a 'coloured' ex-South African to visit South Africa with the MCC team. D'Oliveira was selected as a last-minute replacement for Tom Cartwright, who withdrew because of injury. Vorster refused to accept what he called 'the team of the Anti-Apartheid Movement' and the tour by the English team was cancelled. South Africa was on its way to becoming the polecat of the world. In 1966/67 South Africa had beaten Bobby Simpson's Australian team 3-1 in a Test series, and in 1970 Ali Bacher, with great cricketers like Denis Lindsay, Mike Procter and Graeme Pollock led South Africa to a 4-0 whitewash of Bill Lawry's team. And then South Africa was banned from international cricket.

The moment that defined the end of my cricketing career was not politics but lions. At the end of 1976 we participated in the local derby game of cricket at Skukuza in the Kruger National Park. On our return to Londolozi, after more than our fair share of refreshing beverages, we located a pride of lions in our headlights. As John turned, so that our lights would follow the cats as they crossed the road, he hit a drainage hump, the battery terminal became partly disconnected and the engine stalled. We were in the middle of nowhere surrounded by a large pride of lions that were showing an interest in us. All we could see in the dim head light were yellow eyes staring menacingly at us.

There was a bit of an altercation. In the circumstances, I could have been excused for blurting out, 'What the hell did you do that for?'

However, I was the little brother and I was told to get out and fix the damned thing.

'What about the lions? I asked.

'Chase them away,' was John's retort.

I opened the door and reached for something to throw at the lions. My hand found my cricket kit. So one after another the pads, the bat and the box followed. The box hit a lioness squarely on the head and the last sight I had was of her running off with the box in her mouth.

That was it. As they say in the classics: my cricket career was thrown to the lions. I never again played cricket seriously. My passion for Londolozi overwhelmed all else in my life.

Photograph: Richard du Toit

POLITICS, FENCES AND DISAPPEARING WILDLIFE

We thought we had a simple job ahead of us; invite guests, show them the wonders of our farm, give them the experience and the excitement of walking up to wildlife, take the R3 a day we were charging and wave our happy guests goodbye. But nothing in this life is that simple, as we were soon to discover.

We had no idea that we were about to enter a world full of problems, largely caused by a combination of man's greed and arrogance and the extraordinary mechanisms that politics employs to win the hearts of unsuspecting voters. To paint the picture of the vortex into which we were being drawn, I need to dive back into the mid-19th century.

About 150 years ago hunters from Europe started to come to Africa in their droves. Many people also came to settle only to learn that farming on the southern tip of the African subcontinent was not lucrative in a country plagued by fickle rainfall patterns, hail, cyclones, floods, heat and cold, locust invasions, and devastating diseases which destroyed crops, stock and human life. It became apparent that the easy way to make money was with guns. The Europeans came, they shot and destroyed wildlife and soon moved on. Before the middle of the 19th century, Cape lion, blue buck and quagga were extinct and hippo, which had once been so prolific in the Cape, disappeared south of the Orange River. Frederick Courteney Selous, one of the great hunters of southern Africa, wrote in 1890 that he doubted that there were 20 white rhino left south of the Zambezi.

In the area that became Londolozi, some positive conservation progress was made with the formal establishment of the Sabi Game Reserve in 1902 which was enlarged and proclaimed as the Kruger National Park in 1926. When Colonel James Stevenson-Hamilton became the first warden of the Sabi Game Reserve the antelope populations had been so reduced by 'biltong hunters' that he instructed his game rangers that all predators should be shot on sight so as to re-establish the prey/predator balance. But the worst tragedy of all was that of the elephants. The demand for ivory had so devastated elephant populations that in 1895 only 30 kilograms of ivory were exported from Durban – down from a figure of nearly 20 000 kilograms in 1877. There were almost no elephants left.

Before the turn of the century it was widely recognised that something had to be done about the killing of wildlife. The first game reserve in South Africa – on the Pongola River in KwaZulu-Natal – was proclaimed in 1894 and was followed by many others. However, no thought was given to encompassing complete ecosystems within their boundaries. The repercussions of this oversight were to be felt in the second half of the 20th century. Game reserves all over the country were at the mercy of farmers upstream who abused their water rights and left less and less for users downstream. Nowhere was this more pronounced than with the demarcation of the boundaries of the Kruger National Park which, although it was the largest of all the reserves, was a narrow strip cutting across natural ecological boundaries. Almost nowhere did it include headwaters of rivers.

The phenomenal growth of South Africa's economy – in part driven by the need to become self-sufficient during the years of the Second World War and to help feed the war machine in Europe – and an extractive mentality with its outlook to 'get as much as you can while you can', combined with flawed political ideologies put more pressure on the land and South Africa's unique biodiversity. By the 1970s commercial forests of pine and eucalyptus blanketed the Drakensberg escarpment, while below the mountains row upon row of fruit trees made massive demands on a scarce water resource. Between the lowveld fruit trees and the Kruger Park, relocated people were settled on marginal land and were left to eke out a living from cattle, goats and a handful of mealies. During the drought, many of these farmers lost their stock while erosion cut deeper and deeper fingers into hillsides. The demands on the rivers bringing life to the bushveld increased until eventually the rivers stopped flowing during the winter months. The radical change in the landscape, which was denuded of its protective grass mantle, also led to summer floodwaters tearing down bridges and riverine vegetation – including 100-year-old fig trees – while precious topsoil was carried down to the Indian Ocean where, at river mouths, the mud spread into the ocean like a long brown tongue. The result was a massive decline in the productivity and biodiversity of the coastal plain between the Drakensberg and the Indian Ocean.

Everywhere were signs of drying out and weakening ecosystems which, if allowed to continue, would result in the land becoming less and less productive. In the bushveld some wildlife species like sable and tsessebe disappeared altogether and these selective grass feeders gave way to impala and large mammals such as elephant and buffalo, which have a wide feeding range.

Since the turn of the 20th century, the wildlife within the Kruger Park and the neighbouring private game reserves had not only been preserved but had actually increased in numbers. Now, with the drying up of the rivers, everything was endangered – particularly the unique biodiversity of the bushveld.

Ever since the early 1960s, when veterinary government officials had strung a fence separating the Kruger Park from the private reserves to the west, we had been aware of changes on our beautiful farm. Although this fence was ostensibly put up for veterinary reasons, it was in fact built for military purposes. The Kruger Park was to become a military base in the face of advancing communism down the east coast of the African continent.

To the dismay of everyone, including the Kruger Park officials, the fence caused havoc, killing over 18 000 wildebeest. The fence disrupted their annual migration in search of food and many of the wildebeest died of starvation on the wire because they could not reach their winter grazing across the Sand River. It was to be more than 30 years before the fence was removed. But even now, nearly 50 years later, the western wildebeest population of the Kruger National Park has not recovered.

As a 12-year-old boy I rode the fence line between the Sabi Sand Game Reserve and the Kruger Park with my hero Harry Kirkman. Only the year before he had been savaged by a wounded lion. When he got home he called his doctor and asked, 'Have you got anything for lion bite?' A year later he was back fighting with the KNP officials. He had been promised that if he completed the western fence of the private game reserve before the KNP built their fence, the Sabi Sand would be incorporated into the Kruger Park. But the veterinary officials, using three fencing teams against his one, reached the boundary between the Kruger and the Sabi Sand long before Harry was able to close his western fence. He bemoaned the fact that it was not fair competition and now there was this terrible fence between wildlife and wildlife. That day we saw 400 buffalo just inside the Kruger Park.

With a glint in his eye, Harry brought out wire-cutters and cut the fence. He and I chased the buffalo into the Sabi Sand, closing the fence

Photograph: Heidi Lee Stöckenstrom

Silting rivers due to catchment mismanagement.
The Eastern Lowveld, described as a drying paradise, and the demise of
the selective grass feeders - tsessebe.

behind them. This herd founded the vibrant buffalo population which still exists in the Sabi Sand today.

At Sparta the initial compaction of soils and the downgrading of the system may have been caused by cattle ranching which finally collapsed in 1938 when foot-and-mouth disease devastated the bushveld herds. However, after the game fence was erected, an unnaturally large number of migrating animals were trapped within the relatively small area of the Sabi Sand. This further compacted the soils and hastened the drying out process. Slowly, the wetlands and the open savannah grasslands disappeared while bush encroachment became a major factor.

Yet another example of the dark footprint of apartheid soon followed. Under this dreadful ideology, Bantustan reservations were being created on our western border for black people forcibly removed from the cities. It was intended that they would eventually become independent countries. They would have had no infrastructure, no real source of income and no hope for the people to rise above subsistence levels. The patchwork of landownership and inappropriate land usage of these people, unskilled and untrained in farming, slowly destroyed this great open ecosystem. The flawed apartheid policy of relocating urban people on impoverished land inevitably led to the establishment of communities in which poverty, illiteracy and AIDS would prevail.

To top it all, with the dawning of 1973 a letter from government authorities arrived advising us that consideration was being given to the inclusion of farms in the Sabi Sand Reserve into the neighbouring Bantustan homeland areas of Lebowa and Gazankulu. Two of the farms which faced expropriation were part of the Mala Mala group while two others, Othawa and Ravenscourt were part of Londolozi's traversing area. Halving the size of the Sabi Sand would have been the end of the private game reserve which already suffered from the fence erected in the 60s which cut off migrations from the Kruger Park. Worse still, homeland development, which brings overgrazing and degradation of the land, was to prove to be the ruin of the biodiversity of this once productive area and would make the land virtually valueless.

Fortunately, two influential owners of property in the Sabi Sand, Ian Mackenzie and Jaap Wilkens, visited the prime minister and persuaded him that the expropriation of the farms would be a national tragedy. This triggered in the minds of two young idealistic students who had inherited one of these bushveld farms, the idea that wildlife could be

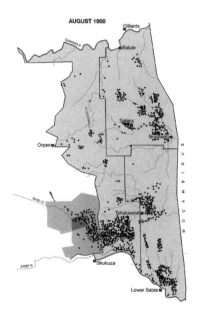

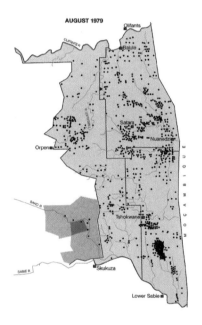

Fences between wildlife and wildlife became a thing of the past.
Two maps based on Ian Whyte's report illustrate the disappearance of
the western wildebeest population of the Kruger Park: 1960, before the
fence was closed and 1979 after 18 000 animals were lost. Black dots
represent the numbers of wildebeest.

economically viable. In fact, by 2007 the tourism industry was generating more revenue than gold in South Africa. The Sabi Sand Game Reserve alone earned over R340 million annually and the value of the land had escalated to over R50 000 per hectare, while on the other side of the hill the former 'homeland' areas' land had become less and less productive and virtually worthless under the prevailing land-use practice.

To the west, the ideology of apartheid was a threat to our dreams. To the east, another ideology, even more frightening, was on the move. Only 40 kilometres from Londolozi, Mozambique was erupting into a battleground with South Africa backing the Renamo forces against the Marxist Frelimo government which took over Mozambique in 1975 with the support of the Russian Bear. Within a decade Mozambique was changed from a safari paradise into the poorest country in the world. Many refugees crossed the narrow section of the Kruger Park directly opposite Londolozi and found their way into our camp. An untold number of people did not arrive at all.

To top it all the Soweto Riots of 1976 resulted in increased sanctions and the beginning of the disinvestment campaign. Landing rights for South African Airways were systematically cancelled throughout the world and almost overnight South Africa became a difficult place to sell as a destination for international travellers. Added to this, 1978 saw the start of a severe drought and the great African theatre that had been part of our lives for so many years slowly disappeared in front of our eyes. The land stretching from the Drakensberg escarpment to the Indian Ocean coastal plain had once been a rich wilderness paradise. We were now beginning to reap the consequences of its turbulent history during which the subtle, but vital linkages, that had created this ecosystem of such vibrancy were slowly destroyed.

We wanted our farm as it had been: a land where animals had the right of way, where the rivers flowed throughout the year and where people of different cultures lived peacefully together. And where the beauty was such that it drove a deep love and determination to understand more about our natural world. It was against this background that Londolozi began searching for solutions.

TAKING OFF – BUT!

A newsletter dated 5 December 1975, written by John and me and addressed to Londolozi's friends, captures our feelings at the time – passionate, idealistic and driven by a strong belief in conservation:

After being involved in wildlife for the last three years and having made it our career, we would like to make our views, ideals and goals known. Our efforts have been geared at improving conditions for people. I believe the time is now right to do something for wild animals in their fight for survival.

We cannot accept that man's population explosion, greed and progress will one day spell ruin to areas like Sabi Sand and its animals. We cannot accept that Sabi Sand will one day be part of Gazankulu, or Lisbon Estates or turned into factories or polluted with comic books and beer cans. The three years with wildlife and its people have sickened us. Indeed, the professional jealousies, the internal politics, the red tape and the breakdown of communications are some of the biggest hindrances facing wildlife today.

We pledged publicly on the 21st October 1975 to do something constructive for wild animals and that we would not allow red tape and people to block our ideals. The five cheetah awaiting transportation are proof of our sincerity. Indeed, if we were men of means with 15 years business experience behind us we would finance the scheme ourselves. However, at 25 and 21 years old we don't feel equipped and confident enough to handle the vast sums of money needed for the project we have in mind.

As I said, we had the answers to all the problems. How prophetic was this newsletter to become. Our first instinct in our search for solutions was to replace lost animals, moving them from other parts of Africa – especially from areas where they were persecuted: cheetah from Namibia's farmlands, leopards from the farming areas of the north-west Transvaal, sable from war-torn Rhodesia, nyala from Ndumu in KwaZulu-Natal where they flourished because there were so few predators, and not least of all elephants from the Kruger Park where they were culled.

John was devastated when some of the Sabi Sand cheetah broke through the fence

A flimsy wooden crate inadequate for a two-ton elephant

line on the west boundary of the Sabi Sand and were shot by government officials. With the deaths of these cats, the cheetah population of the Sabi Sand was down to two. So it was to cheetah that we first turned our attention.

We formed the Londolozi Game Reserve Trust – a not-for-profit organisation – and Shan, the 'Wednesday legs' girl, together with a band of schoolboys she enrolled for the task, sold crayfish and raffle tickets door-to-door in Johannesburg. She raised R15 000 – enough to get five cheetah flown in from Namibia. But John felt we needed more: more of all the animals we no longer saw. We also wanted to know why the animals had disappeared.

Then John went to Kenya in search of solutions. He met some special people in conservation like George Adamson, well-known for his love of lions, David Hopcroft, a leading authority on how to use wildlife commercially and sustainably, and Bill Woodley who provided a number of insights into ways in which natural systems work and fit together. What John learnt from them became key ingredients of the Londolozi model. He also heard elephants described as second only to man as agents to habitat change. Building on this, John came back with a theory that we should introduce elephants – lots of them – as they would solve our problem of bush encroachment and result in the natural restoration of our grasslands and wetlands. The five elephants left in the Sabi Sand after the fence was closed were not enough.

We approached the Kruger Park authorities with our normal exuberance, stepping unwittingly into the rigid and intolerant Kruger arena and making the outrageous suggestion that culling was not necessary and that relocation was the answer to their problem of rapidly increasing elephant populations.

'Instead of culling elephants, why not move them,' we suggested. We had space for them and to our mind relocation was a viable option.

We got nowhere. The Kruger authorities viewed themselves as an island of absolute authority. They excluded the private parks, shunned private enterprise and considered that they were not responsible to neighbouring rural communities. Clearly, we were an uncomfortable development in the isolated environment of the Kruger National Park whose officials were not used to being questioned on their conservation policies. We did, however, find common ground with Dr Tol Pienaar, the head of the KNP, whose love of wildlife was equal to our own and who listened to our ideas. He stuck his neck out and told us that if we got veterinary permission to move the elephants he would help us.

It was the loophole we were looking for. We had it on the best authority (our old friend Harry Kirkman who knew everything there was to know about the National Parks hierarchy) that Pienaar was a man of his word. So we marched on Pretoria. As it happened, the head of veterinary services was new to his job. He had not formed any opinion on the bunch of young upstarts from Londolozi with all the answers to all the questions. We stated our case and he gave us the necessary veterinary permission to move the elephants. Two weeks later we were back in Dr Pienaar's office with the veterinary permit in our hands. As we anticipated, Dr Pienaar was committed to the process and soon after that the first ever elephant relocation out of the Kruger National Park was under way.

Suddenly we had a marvellous group of new friends, many of whom were dedicated to conservation. From Bruce Bryden, head ranger of the Kruger, down, none of the field men had enjoyed culling elephants. They were really excited and could hardly believe that these 'bloody youngsters' from across the fence had convinced their bosses to open up this new frontier in conservation for them.

We went through a steep learning curve moving the first batch of young elephants. The date was 5 November 1978 and the temperature in the helicopter was 42 degrees centigrade at nine in the morning. Back in the 1950s and 1960s, the groundwork on the M99 capture drug had been laid by Dr Ian Player when he relocated both black and white rhinos from Umfolozi. But the Kruger Park capture team was now working with a much larger mammal. Because it was a pioneering project, there was an element of guesswork in the amount of the M99 capture drug darted into each mammal. We were also soon to learn that the sable crates adapted to carry the juvenile elephants were completely inadequate – even with all the reinforcing we had done. The result was chaotic. When the first young elephant that had been captured was given the antidote, she took a deep breath and, screaming in juvenile rage, shattered the flimsy crate around her. In the blink of an eyelid, the two-ton baby on one end of the rope had the 25 men on the other end scattering in all directions. It was a miracle that no one was hurt and that afterwards we could laugh about it. Despite the bad start, eight young elephants were relocated that day.

Once again, John was on a roll. Eight elephants were not enough. They were seldom seen at Londolozi. He wanted more. And, by extension, our thoughts turned to how we could find the money to pay for them. Our search took us to the New York office of the producer of ABC Network Television's Sportsmen's Programme. He was a typical film man with the attention span of a hummingbird. His phone rang non-stop during our meeting and it was difficult to get his attention. The idea of catching elephants in South Africa – the land of apartheid 6 500 miles away – was not a priority for the man 'from Hollywood'.

In his desperation John jumbled his words and said that we would dart helicopters from elephants! At that the producer slowed down and said, 'Say that again.'

For a moment we had his attention and John corrected himself, saying he would dart elephants from helicopters and then sling them under the chopper to move them to their new habitat. I could not believe my ears. Never before had anyone tried to hang an elephant under a helicopter. But I could see that the producer, whose business it was to think in pictures, was intrigued and was formulating a spectacular film sequence in his mind. There was no doubt he thought it would make good television viewing.

The meeting ended with an agreement that ABC Network America would pay for the relocation of the elephants in South Africa in exchange for the film rights. Their two-hour sportsmen's programme was formatted around a celebrity taken into the wild somewhere in the world and letting him or her be part of the adventure. Our celebrities were the beautiful Cheryl Tiegs – the highest paid model in the world – and the high-profile Ben Abruzzo, who had hit the headlines when he made the first ever solo crossing of the Atlantic Ocean in a helium balloon in 1978. Our job was to create a spectacular film sequence and an adventure story.

This is what we did. We moved 25 elephants in the most chaotic, thrilling and amusing venture I have ever participated in.

Can you imagine Cheryl Tiegs checking her make-up before facing the camera to host the show? There were two helicopters with their pilots and Kruger Park sharp-shooters ready to take off; hot-air balloons under the command of Ben Abruzzo; 18 film crew members; professional stills photographers with their extra-long lenses; magazine journalists; National Park section rangers and labourers; state veterinary officials; truck and crane drivers and many idle bystanders. It could only be described as an African-style 'rodeo'. And then, with the ABC director John Wilcox waiting impatiently, Ben Pretorius, a marvellous Kruger National Park section ranger and the man in ultimate charge of the operation, opened his game-capture box to discover that he had left the M99 capture drug back in the fridge at his house in Skukuza, 300 kilometres to the south – too far away to fetch that day. The cost of the day's filming was lost and if it wasn't hot enough, John Wilcox, lost his patience and sent the temperature skyrocketing. The next day it all worked like a charm. Wilcox got his pictures and we got 25 more elephants.

Sitting around the campfire at the end of that exhausting day was a medley of people from many different walks of life. The party included Ben Pretorius and other Kruger Park rangers, our Londolozi team and Dr Ken Tinley, who was prepared to challenge anybody on conservation issues. Equally vocal was the adventurous Ben Abruzzo, Cheryl Tiegs and her boyfriend, Peter Beard, an even more radical conservationist from Kenya and the author of a thought-provoking book, *The End of the Game*. It was a group of massive egos and everyone wanted to air his or her views.

Inevitably the conversation turned to elephants. Too many? Too few? To cull? Not to cull? Somewhere between midnight and dawn, through a haze of too much whisky and the self-belief that develops after a wildly successful day, a new plan was hatched. Peter Beard came up with a proposal to raise funds for elephants by taking over Studio 54, the New York nightclub which was so in demand that even stars had to queue to get in. He said he would persuade the owner, Steve Rubell, to donate the money taken at the gate for the night to the cause of elephants. For us it was the unreachable and we were pretty wide-eyed and disbelieving. But we were not going to be left out and had quite a bit to say. Then Cheryl suggested that she would ask Mick Fleetwood, her personal friend and leader of the sensational rock band Fleetwood Mac, to provide the music. Cheryl and Peter Beard, high-profile New Yorkers, would host the evening. And this was what actually happened.

Peter, who was already designing the cover of the *Tusk* album for Fleetwood Mac, designed the invitation and decorated Studio 54 with an elephant theme. The elephant-sized invitation, measuring nearly a metre across, was sent to the cream of New York society – and the evening was oversubscribed tenfold.

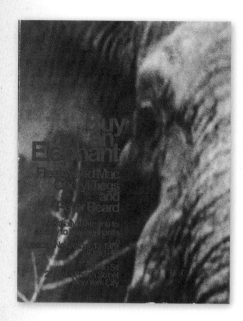

Rock stars, fashion models and elephants

Picture the scene: the boys from Africa in the heart of New York raising money for elephants. Yes, we got the gate for the night and we captured a two-hour slot on Network Television across America on the sportsmen programme. But there were a couple of problems. The costs mounted and we found ourselves with a bill of $67 000. The next morning we couldn't find the owner of Studio 54 to collect our money. We thought he had disappeared. As it turned out, we kept very different schedules and in the middle of the afternoon he arrived. But he told us that the gate for the evening had amounted to only $69 000. It seemed that he was not as dedicated to the cause of saving elephants as we had hoped. Of course we were angry but came down to earth when our old friend Tedd Schorman advised us to cool it. He told us, 'Be careful guys. In New York for $1 000 you can have a car blown up and for $2 000 they can have you in it!'

Nonetheless, even if we did not make much money, the publicity was enormous and out of it came a whole new interest in the elephants of Africa from the world of film and rock stars. We found ourselves talking to people like Peter Sellers, Tina Turner, Spike Milligan, the Irish folk-singer Chris de Burgh, Chicago, and Blood, Sweat and Tears, to name a few.

More importantly for conservation, the Kruger National Park rangers laid the foundation for the relocation of elephants safely and humanely to other parts of southern Africa. Since 1978 they have improved their techniques and more than 2 000 elephants, including mature bulls, have been relocated to the Eastern Cape, Pilanesberg, Maputaland and Mozambique, among other places. Elephants have become the great new symbol of advancing green frontiers in Africa through the development of transfrontier parks and the reopening of migratory corridors. Nonetheless, the elephant debate remains as emotive and complicated as ever. It is a question of space. People want the land. Elephants need the land. Who will win?

Our Studio 54 story had one more twist in its tail. When John and I went to New York, we left 'The Girls' – Shan, John's girlfriend Vee Maskill, and Janine Ovendale – in South Africa to mind 'The Shop'. The girls had worked their fingers to the bone looking after the film crew, stitching up Ben Abruzzo's balloons when they got snagged in thorn trees, running non-stop to feed everyone and keep the whole team happy. When we flew to New York and they were not invited, they got the hell in. Under the leadership of the naughty, mischievous and miffed Shan, they decided that they would have their own Studio 54 bush party. We only heard about it on our return. Without our permission they closed Londolozi for three days (an unprecedented event), and organised a non-stop party that became legendary throughout the Lowveld. When I came back from America I stopped in Nelspruit to get supplies and told the guy to charge the bill to Londolozi.

He looked at me in awe: 'Londolozi,' he said. 'That's where they had that party?' The girls had spread Londolozi's fame across the Lowveld.

With the continued support of Cheryl Tiegs and Peter Beard and with wonderful contributions from Spike Milligan and Peter Sellers, we continued to relocate elephants through the Londolozi Game Trust and in April 1983 wrote to our friends:

Our elephant introduction programmes are bearing fruit and our aerial count records 42 elephants for Sabi Sand.

A year later we reported that: *Good news in the elephant world is that a calf has been born to the nine-year-old elephant which was relocated to Londolozi four years ago.*

At the same time, but from further afield, we reported that:

The eight elephants donated by the Londolozi Game Trust have all settled down well in the Pilanesberg Game Reserve.

In retrospect, it was ridiculous that we had to put the elephants through the traumatic experience of being relocated. We destroyed their family structure (because we knew no better and did not have the ability in those days to relocate an adult matriarch or bull elephant). Our action completely disrupted all forms of succession and communication within the herd, and we had to hold the elephants in a boma for veterinary reasons before finally releasing the poor little buggers into a completely strange area which was, anyway, ecologically linked to where they came from. We took baby elephants away from their families thinking we were doing a good thing. We did not understand the consequences.

We embarked on elephant relocation for a multitude of reasons – some good and some bad. We were passionate about getting elephants back into Londolozi and I believe we were correct. But the circumstances that led to our decision – the fence between wildlife and wildlife – and the culling which was the alternative to taking it down was lunacy. After 1992 when the fence was finally removed, the land between the Sabi and Sand Rivers which is known as the Sabi Sand Reserve went from 60 elephants in 1993 to 300 elephants in 1995 to 500 elephants in 1996, to 700 elephants in 1999 and to nearly 1 000 by 2007. The elephants did not need man to tell them where to go for their winter grazing.

The same thing could happen between the Kruger Park and Mozambique. Just take down the fence and have patience. The elephants will go back if they find grazing, water and peace. They once belonged in the east. We don't have to spend millions of rands and put elephants through such a traumatic experience and in some instances kill them in the process. First create the space and then wait and see what nature does.

Photograph: Gavin Joyce

BACK ON TRACK

W̶e felt that we had come a long way since we had opened our doors to guests, with Shan handling all the bookings from the attic of her parents' home and David Lawrence taking the promotional side on 'his broad shoulders'. In December 1974 we wrote our second ever newsletter: *Due to considerably increased costs, we have regretfully been compelled to increase our charges to R15 per night slept – with children under 10 at half price.*

Also in the newsletter we wrote:

Londolozi has finally given up the unequal struggle of trying to keep drop toilets hygienic especially when the temperature gets around 100 degrees. The result is a flush toilet with hot and cold showers and a bath for the ladies. For those who still want to remain close to nature, the drop toilets and the open-air showers remain.

Four years later we wrote to our friends advising that Londolozi's rates for '*Rustic rondavels are increasing to R37 per person per night and R59 for our fully inclusive luxury chalets*'. We thought we were doing well! Retirement and riches were just around the bend. And in 1983 I reached the peak of my copywriting ability in our year-end newsletter; '*sightings of young cheetah, wild dog, hyena and lion have been recorded and leopards have been spotted!*' (My friend, Paul Bannister, never let me forget that one.)

Despite our success, we were still searching for answers to the many complex conservation and land management issues we faced. In particular, the disappearance and decline of certain species was, for us, a matter of great concern. Eventually Dr Ken Tinley was able to help us. When John heard of him we were getting desperate. Yes, he was a professional and had a doctorate in wildlife management. But he had something else. Unlike other experts we consulted, his ideas were formulated on the ground by incredible powers of observation. He understood landscape patterns, geomor-phology and the broader macro-issues of conservation development and the need to involve rural communities. He understood how to repair Londolozi's land which, like the surrounding area, was drying out. Ken asked us to locate

Outdoor bush basin - bushveld camp life, 1973

Before and after. Clearing the bush in order to raise the water table. Twenty years later Dave returns with his mentor, Ken Tinley, to see the results.

the 1944 aerial photographs of our land. When he arrived he spent the day looking at them and then asked us to take him to various points marked on the map. When we sat down with him that evening, he explained what had happened. Referring frequently to the notebook he carried with him, he explained how the landscape had once been a pattern of mosaic woodlands and grasslands and how it had changed. It was a revelation. Like turning the pages of a book, Ken laid the story before our eyes.

He told us exactly how, over the past century, man had damaged the natural environment. Man had brought in cattle, had built roads and even a railway line. Many of the roads and tracks and even fire-breaks acted like funnels accelerating the run-off of rainwater because they were built straight down hillsides or on the seepline (a layer of sand sitting directly above clays which would hold moisture). We had also come in on the back-end of a cattle ranching operation and much of the topsoil had been compacted by cattle, particularly at water points. The explosion in the wildebeest population and the confinement of many thousands of these animals within the Sabi Sand when the fence was closed in 1964, had exacerbated the problem. The result was that instead of rainwater soaking into the ground, it ran off, and where the natural ground cover had disappeared, it took topsoil with it. When the water table dropped and the land dried out, trees and woody shrubs invaded the grasslands and the wetlands disappeared.

Tinley was quite brutal with us. He told us that we reminded him of all conservationists: 'You want to get your picture on the social page because you're going to save cheetah and elephants,' he would say. 'That's the biggest load of bullshit I've ever heard. Don't save the animals. They don't need saving. Protect your land from bad land-use practices, create space for the animals and they will thrive.'

The first night he was with us we served him roast lamb for dinner. He nearly had an apoplexy. 'Why are you giving this to me in the middle of a game reserve?' he said. 'Give me an impala steak. Don't you know that we have 97 different ungulate species in Africa? Far more than any other continent. You don't need cattle, sheep and goats. Look what they do to your land. Africa's wildlife has been designed for this harsh continent. Use it wisely. Eat it. Why should the people of Africa die amidst plenty?'

His next point was that we should always look beyond our own borders and that we should share the benefits of wildlife with those who had less.

'You cannot expect to be an island of prosperity amid a sea of poverty,' he told us. He also told us to look outside the reserve. 'That's where your threats lie. This river is being destroyed upstream.' He added, 'Nature is your partner. Work with her.'

Now we had something to run with and we quickly got down to work. Using an aerial map, Ken showed us where things had gone wrong and where we would have to clear tree species that had invaded the open grasslands: how the great natural plan of the ecosystem had been altered by man's intervention. He showed us how we could micro-manage our little patch for greater biodiversity and greater drought resistance. To do so we would have to close up the eroded ravines and create grassed waterways, reroute roads and redirect or close the firebreaks. We had only to consider the water table. By reducing run-off we could ensure that the rainwater soaked into the soil and that the soil moisture balance was raised. It was a radical and controversial approach to wilderness conservation and it was a gigantic task. But we were totally committed and despite being desperately under-capitalised, we embarked on 'The Tinley Plan'.

We started hacking the trees out by hand. Then Ross Parry-Davies, who had first helped us with our waterborne sewerage and who had became a great friend, returned for his annual safari to Londolozi. He brought a friend of his, Dr Zac de Beer, who happened to be the CEO of the biggest construction company in South Africa, a subsidiary of Anglo American called LTA.

Again we told our story and the challenges we faced. Two or three weeks later a brand new D5 yellow bulldozer arrived at Londolozi. We had it on loan for five weeks. We rigged up lights and worked night and day. BP also helped by donating diesel. The trees came down, the dongas were plugged and soon the wetlands that had dried up started to fill with water. The water table rose. Then the game started to reappear. The great turning point for us was seeing the first leopard on our land for over a decade. There was huge excitement. Our partner was playing her part.

The relationship with LTA and BP – between the industrial world and the natural world – turned out to be highly successful. The dams we built with their help created theatre in the bush. The return of mosaic grasslands and woodlands brought back a diversity of antelope and the predators followed. This was when the seed of linking big business and conservation, to their mutual benefit, was born.

Once we started to care for our land, nature responded and we were in an upward, virtuous cycle. Game viewing became so much better and drives covered less than half the distance. In a single afternoon guests would watch lions, hyena and vultures for hours, see giraffe browsing on the trees or buffalo and rhinoceros grazing nearby, as well as an infinite number of antelope. For nearly a decade we spent more money on our land than we made out of our fledgling safari business. But we were becoming known as a great wildlife destination – especially after John followed a female leopard which was tolerant of our vehicles. Night after night for nearly two years John filmed her with her cubs and finally in a fatal confrontation with a pride of lions.

This mother leopard and her progeny became our star attraction. We were inundated with guests from all over the world who wanted to see the Londolozi leopards. Our safari model was taking shape and, in turn, a whole new range of opportunities opened to us. This was the embryonic stage of a new and enduring partnership with animals, ambassadors if you will, from the natural world.

John and I built Londolozi by instinctively working out our own roles and our different contributions. Almost inadvertently we came up with a textbook management formula with each partner providing unique contributions. We had role clarity, aligned interests and a diversity of talents which added up to a successful operation. John did the land and the conservation, he became this maverick film-maker from Londolozi and was soon off on his own journey. He did things that some people thought total madness, but because they were controversial, they made interesting stories. John was always way ahead with new ideas. He also took the trouble to visit people all over the world. He learnt from curators of zoos in America, from game wardens in India and especially from the people of East Africa where he did a lot of filming.

On the flip side of the coin, Shan and I were the owner-managers. We drove the business by making sure the bills were paid, the beds were clean and the guests kept coming. There is no more successful a way of marketing a safari lodge than having an excited, thrilled-to-bits departing guest. And we had an abundance of happy guests who returned again and again.

The third person behind the scene at Londolozi was our rock-solid partner Allan Taylor. Allan was a true friend to both John and me and his commitment in believing that we would make the grade was – in

Four generations of Taylor. Frank Unger (above) and his daughter Betty Taylor (top). Allan Taylor (right), Frank Unger's grandson, and two great grandchildren.

no small measure – part of the reason for Londolozi's success. Although our grandfathers, Charles Varty and Frank Unger, had bought the farm together way back in 1926, Allan had little to do with Londolozi in the early years. His mother, Betty Taylor – who eventually inherited half of Sparta – had left South Africa for Australia and it was only on her return to South Africa in the early 1970s that we again met up with Allan.

Betty Taylor had been approached by our eastern neighbour with an offer of a long-term exclusive lease of her bushveld asset – a catastrophic development which would have severely limited any future prospects for Londolozi as a viable business, particularly as the lease included an option to purchase the farm. Before signing the lease, she decided to have a meeting with us and she brought Allan with her. She also brought her family trustees and some heavy legal advisers. The neighbour had proposed building a luxury lodge on the Taylor property and paying a lucrative guaranteed annual rental. We were in no position to make a counter offer. We were totally despondent because we were dependent on the Taylor land to ensure the viability of our game viewing and we planned to build Bush Camp on the Unger-Taylor property. Before taking her final decision Betty asked Allan what he would like to do: 'After all, if we keep it, it will be your inheritance one day.' Allan's reply came out of the doom and gloom of the meeting like a thunderbolt: 'I think we should stick with the Vartys,' he told his mother. 'We came here together, we should stay together. Please don't sign the lease.' The legal advisers went ballistic. On the table was a rock-solid offer while John and I, scarcely out of our teens, were suggesting that we would build a bush camp for the 'client', 'made of mud.'

Allan could not have been a more ideal partner: he made his assets and his money available and let us get on with the job. We reported to him as a non-executive partner. But when the Londolozi business needed something he was there for us. What more could anyone ask for in any relationship? We had trust and faith in one another and shared a wonderful friendship and desire to conserve the beautiful wilderness for posterity. After 29 years together we decided to draw up a shareholders' agreement so that we would have a record of what we had agreed all those years earlier under a marula tree.

A CONSERVATION MODEL IS BORN

The lessons of the 1970s endure to this day. At Londolozi there was no strong central control. Managers, owners, shareholders and rangers were all as one. If one guy stepped out of line and did not look after his guests, all his mates would let him know in no uncertain terms. When a guest arrived all the staff showed up – dressed for the event in their scruffy cut-off jeans, torn shirts and beards. There was no red carpet, but their warmth and enthusiasm made guests feel like royalty. Game drives were often extended for hours to follow a leopard and her cubs or a pride on the hunt. Rangers took guests with them to research the game, an extra walk, an extra chat and the opportunity to become involved in all the activities of the safari lodge – even a game of soccer with staff.

What was magical was that we were one big family and when guests arrived at Londolozi, they became part of that family. We had a common goal and an energy that was supercharged. We did anything. There was no hierarchy. No food and beverage manager. No front of house manager or guest relations manager. No regulations. No layers. We were jacks of all trades. At one stage Shan was receptionist, typist, bookkeeper, telephone operator, entertainment organiser and stores clerk. We believed that if we could dream it, we could do it.

There was no need for us to motivate our staff. We were a groundswell of people who had ideas that had merit. People got up before dawn and went to bed late. Between their game viewing, research and walking with guests everyone had a special project. Tony Adams photographed the land every year to monitor the habitat. We decided we would be our own aerial photographers and modified a camera stand which we welded to the front seat of a Cessna 182 so that, with the door removed and the new seat in position, the camera would face directly downwards. It was a Heath Robinson affair and with my 100-hours flying time and possibly a lot of courage from Tony who had to hang out the plane, we went and gridded the whole of Londolozi. It was a pioneering approach

Dave shows his commitment to doing whatever it took to care for guests.

Chief pilots of the 'white knuckle' charter compnay, Shan and Dave.
An elephant modifies our plane.

to monitoring the habitat and we weren't all that good at flying straight lines, with the result that sometimes we had overlapping pictures and at other times we left areas out. But we thought we were doing a great job until satellite photography came into being.

Paddy Hagelthorn had a scheme for every minute of the day. He was into guineafowl breeding but especially into fish: he was going to produce enough protein from this scheme to feed the whole of Africa. I agreed that he should make four tanks for his barbel to test the project. To my absolute amazement it worked and before long we had 32 tanks filled with 110 000 barbel. Then one morning we had 110 000 dead barbel. Something had gone wrong and that was the end of Londolozi's fishing industry.

Everyone got involved in forwarding our model of care, especially care of the community. We tried to show people how to help themselves. Shan had a vegetable patch – this was a really long story and nearly ended our otherwise harmonious relationship. Another started a sewing group, repairing linen and making uniforms for the camp. Because everyone worked beyond the confines of self, far from having a high staff turnover, nobody left. It was the most magical place in the world and was regarded as home by all who worked there.

All of us felt that those early years at Londolozi were the best days of our lives. Why? It was, I believe, because we had found a cause – a common purpose and a passion. It went far beyond a job and was much more fulfilling. To be in an industry that is self-sustaining and in partnership with nature had so much more meaning than to be in an extractive industry which comes to an end when the resource is either finished or destroyed. Those who have the good fortune to become involved in a family business that is successful and sustainable are the recipients of a rare gift that should be cherished and preserved.

All this became known as the 'Londolozi Experience'. We built up an ethos of involving and having fun with our guests and seeing our operations through their eyes, as opposed to serving our convenience. We were passionate about service excellence and it was central to everything we did. We borrowed concepts from many different service establishments: 'Moments of Truth' was coined by Scandinavian Airlines in the 1960s to identify key contact points in the chain of a guest experience. Then we drew up guidelines: the importance of the 'Third-eye' which aimed to develop the ability to walk into a room and to see what was out of place.'The $2000 rule' came from the Ritz/Carlton Hotel of London. We gave our staff the liberty to spend R2 000 for a guest's immediate needs without checking with anyone. We would tell our staff to take on-the-spot decisions to keep guests happy. They were not to be told, 'No, I can't help you,' or 'I'll get back to you.' We used the platform of the 'Great African theatre' to take our guests beyond anything they could ever have experienced. And so this little bush camp unwittingly married international first world standards of service with the splendour of wild Africa. The simple rules we drew up then are as important today as ever.

The bush personalities who we grew up with at Londolozi and with whom we shared a passion for the African wilderness, have today largely been replaced by hoteliers and professional guides. The result has been that much of the spontaneity of the bush safari lodge experience has been replaced by the more staid 'professionalism' found in a hotel – perhaps inevitable as the industry has matured.

In those early years the driving force of our bush experience was the energy of nature and the beauty of wildlife. To us, cuisine, the size of the room and the intriguing decor were all subordinate but supportive to the adventure. We were never in danger of allowing a hotel manager's 'tail' become so important that it wagged the wildlife 'dog'. We lived in a beautiful and exciting corner of the world and we wanted to share the gift of nature that was our inheritance. Our purpose was to involve guests in the endless fascination of nature, to provide the opportunity for our guests to learn and always to ensure that they had fun.

Susie Cazenove recorded in her book, *Licensed to Guide*, the occasion when Londolozi guests were greeted by a pilot dressed in a gorilla suit eating bananas at the Skukuza Airport. 'Scratching his armpits and grunting, he herded them into a plane and as he climbed in he put his earphones over his arm and held up a book with large letters on the front: *How to fly a Plane*, asking if any of them could help start the plane.' It is this wonderful sense of fun that permeated any visit to Londolozi.

The 1980s started with our friend Steve Fitzgerald commenting that our game experience was more exciting, more informed and more genuinely involved than any of our competitors. But, he did not mince his words in telling us what he thought of our hospitality. 'All you need to do is to fix your hospitality and you'll be the best.'

Then Steuart Pennington, who had come out of wage bargaining and union negotiations while working at Anglo American, told us, 'You're too busy with your land and your animals and now your hospitality. But you're missing out the key component. Don't forget the political dynamic. Look at the role of black people in a future South Africa.' The Pennington advice came from big industry, trade unions, and politics – a completely different direction to that of Ken Tinley. But the convergence of their ideas became a key component embedded in our conservation model: that of linking our neighbouring communities and staff to the benefits of tourism. Also fundamental to the success of the Londolozi formula was that you must consult with people. There is great wisdom amongst the ancient African cultures and everyone working in rural Africa should understand the importance of collective consultation.

Next, Bobby Lawrence introduced us to Enos Mabuza, chief minister of the independent homeland of KaNgwane, nearby neighbours of Londolozi. Enos listened to our talks about the multi-use of wildlife and how it could benefit rural people all over Africa. Then he directed us towards ways in which we could integrate our staff. Our friendship with Enos soon attracted other interest. Not only was he chief minister. He was also a known member of the ANC and was considered a dangerous communist by the government security forces. He was continually watched and so were we. Nonetheless, we followed his advice and started on the work of integrating our staff at all levels of our operations.

The combination of the inputs of our four friends, Steve Fitzgerald (hospitality), Ken Tinley (land care and neighbourly relations), Enos Mabuza (the political dynamic) and Steuart Pennington (people issues), helped build a model that would stand up anywhere in the world. As we built the model, we met fantastic people, many of whom helped us on our journey. And at Londolozi, the same group of people with their 'if you can dream it, you can do it' culture and their passion and enthusiasm remained. The Londolozi model became the benchmark for an entire industry. It also became a guide for the safari industry in a country which, as a democracy, would soon find its way back onto the world stage.

During the 1980s Shan and I worked hard on the guidelines that had been given us by our friends. We would do everything we could to bring Londolozi hospitality up to world standards. And we would do so with the same group of people who had been with us through thick and thin

from the beginning. Shan went further and decided that we should aim for Relais & Châteaux recognition. It was a tough assignment but after two years of working through the long list of Relais requirements, and upgrading our cuisine with the enthusiastic expertise of Yvonne Short and Trish Marshall (décor), the Relais representatives arrived at Londolozi and we passed with flying colours – the first ever Relais & Châteaux safari lodge in the world.

At Londolozi guests were getting better rooms, better food and better wildlife viewing and the staff was finding more opportunities. There was no doubt that something was working. What emerged was the Londolozi model for conservation development. Our linking of people, wildlife and land together in a hospitality and interpretive wildlife viewing experience was taking shape. We had set the stage to show the world a South Africa that had hope for the future.

Johan Hoekstra 2000

MANDELA

'During my long walk to freedom, I had the rare privilege to visit Londolozi. There I saw people of all races living in harmony amidst the beauty that Mother Nature offers. There I saw a living lion in the wild. Londolozi represents a model of the dream I cherish for the future of nature preservation in our country.' Nelson Mandela, 1995.

Enos Mabuza became a frequent visitor to Londolozi and a good friend. He was a quiet gentleman with a razor-sharp mind and enormous wisdom. In those early years, I did not realise that Enos was to become a man of enormous influence. In our many discussions with him he had often reminded us of the future we faced. 'You must be prepared for the new South Africa under Nelson Mandela,' he told us. 'You must pour the cultures together. Celebrate the differences.' He was profound and his guidance was vital to the creation of the Londolozi model.

In 1990, a huge opportunity and one of the most defining moments in my life started with a phone call from Enos who asked if we would receive a friend of his at Londolozi. Enos continued in his typically understated manner, 'Dave, what I require you to do is to give my friend your views on conservation. He may be able to influence the future conservation policy in South Africa.'

A few days later Nelson Mandela arrived at Londolozi as my private guest. There was no fanfare as I had been asked by Enos to keep the visit low key. There would be no great party, no security, no press and I had no idea what to expect. Madiba had been released from prison a few months earlier and no doubt Enos felt that he would benefit from a few days in the bushveld which has such wonderful therapeutic powers. At the same time Enos gave me a golden opportunity to tell my Londolozi story – a story that was to have a profound effect on the future direction of conservation development in South Africa.

As we set out on our first game drive, we hardly talked at all. I drove and he sat in silence. Then we located a leopard hunting and for the first time in his life Madiba was able to view the beauty of this animal

A turning point for conservation and the dawning of the restoration age in South Africa. Enos Mabuza and artist Bobby Lawrence - the catalysts who opened the window on conservation for Nelson Mandela

in its wild natural habitat. We followed the leopard as it manoeuvred on the hunt. Sometimes we would lose the cat. And then we would find it again. For the most part we were absolutely silent. And then she made a kill. It was the raw drama of the bush that Madiba witnessed for the first time and that people from all over the world come to see.

Afterwards I talked about the great outdoor theatre that South Africa offered the world. That our uniquely African wilderness had huge potential to provide jobs and business opportunities for people and that the land itself would benefit. That tourism could become the core industry driving the economy of South Africa. That we were globally competitive and, unlike mining, this industry would endure forever.

We spoke of the reality of our rivers which were being abused in the name of industry, agriculture and politics. We dreamed of a South Africa whose leaders would provide up-to-date legislation to protect rivers and would legislate for proper environmental assessments before dams were built. We wanted them to ensure that the forestry companies, which had manipulated the situation during the apartheid years and overdeveloped vital catchment areas with commercial plantations, would be brought to task and made to toe the line.

We talked of the need to change entrenched outdated thinking, especially relating to the extraction of so much water from perennial rivers that people and land downstream were deprived of their water resource. We also wanted the government to recognise inappropriate land-use practices that were damaging land and destroying biodiversity. This meant that we were looking at the creation of new parks and the expansion of existing ones on land that had been taken in a downward spiral of degradation by poor farming. We also believed that community participation was essential. We dreamed of a network of wildlife corridors linking existing parks together and turning South Africa into the wildlife destination of the world.

What I found was a man of extraordinary presence with an enquiring mind. Madiba was a great listener and asked a lot of questions. I did not know then that he would remember these discussions with absolute clarity. Madiba promised that once the ANC led the government, tourism would be a top priority. He also promised that he would send other senior ANC members to Londolozi to see how we had created harmony between the different race groups and said that 'Londolozi represents a model of the dream I cherish for the future of our country.'

Nelson Mandela made good on all his promises and South Africa has, since then, significantly advanced the green frontiers in many areas of the country.

A few weeks later five members of the ANC National Executive arrived at Londolozi, one of whom was Thabo Mbeki who would be president when the transfrontier parks were signed off by South Africa and four neighbouring countries. Another visitor was Professor Kader Asmal, Minister of Water Affairs and Forestry in South Africa's first democratically elected government, and a passionate advocate of protecting river catchments. Bruce Babbit, former US Secretary of the Interior, described South Africa's National Water Conservation Campaign as 'unprecedented in terms of approach and effectiveness, anywhere in the world'. Later, I met Valli Moosa who had a profound effect on driving the necessary legislation and cross-border cooperation needed to create transfrontier parks, which would add millions of hectares to wildlife conservation.

Through Enos Mabuza we had found a way to showcase the unique gift we had received from nature. We wanted to share this knowledge with our government and anyone who would listen. We knew we had learnt something special and that if other landowners would put our model to work, land would be used more wisely and the rural people of Africa would benefit.

With the new energies in the southern regions of Africa and supported and encouraged by Madiba, I took my first tentative step in my search for more challenges. On my agenda was Reserva d'Elefantas d'Maputa in the war zone of southern Mozambique. The reserve had been closed for the entire duration of the 20-year civil war. Now that discussions between South Africa and Mozambique were starting, it seemed that there was an opportunity to reopen the reserve where the elephant herds had been decimated and even link the Mozambique reserve with Ndumu Game Reserve and Tembe Elephant Park across the border in South Africa. This area – to the north and south of a relatively new border fence – had been the last domain of free-ranging elephants in the region. Perhaps we could take down the border fence and reinstate their ancient migratory route.

I remember landing on the beach in our helicopter and walking up the path to the front gate of the Ponta do Ouro hotel. It was like a ghost town in an American movie. The doors creaked, there was sand everywhere, the till on the counter was covered with cobwebs and the whole place was deathly silent. It was as if 20 years ago people had left in a hurry. Now there was not a soul around. There could have been landmines anywhere so we decided to get some back-up and return at a later date after the Frelimo army had checked out the area.

A few weeks later we returned in a King Air with the Frelimo commander-in-chief on board. As we approached the runway we could not see any of his ground force who had been instructed to secure the landing strip for our arrival.

As the pilot was preparing to land I said: 'If we can't see people on the ground when they should be there, there must be something wrong.'

I was unwilling to land, so the pilot took us back to Maputo. On their return to Ponta do Ouro later that day to recheck the area, the plane came under fire and they had to make a forced landing to the south at Kosi Bay. I was glad I was not there. Perhaps this was an early warning of the hazards of reopening Africa after the collapse of the various ideologies that had swept through the continent.

I had taken my decision. Londolozi was running on well-oiled wheels. It was rated number one in the world by Condé Nast, it was the first Relais & Châteaux safari lodge in the world, and had just won the British Airways Tourism for Tomorrow Award. It was time for Shan and me to look beyond our small, secure patch and enter the higher university of life.

Photograph: Richard du Toit

EXPORTING THE MODEL

How I came to spend the next 10 years of my life expanding the Londolozi model into the creation of Conservation Corporation Africa (CCAfrica) came about through my brother John. CCAfrica was initially set up to bring business disciplines to conservation and develop the grassroots Phinda Game Reserve in Maputaland. Within a decade the Corporation was operating in five African countries.

John had always been a bit of a ladies' man and seemed to leave a trail of lovely women in his wake. One of these women was a highly articulate, in-your-face conservation journalist from Durban. Jane Conyngham wrote for the *Sunday Tribune*. One of her stories was about a farmer who had bulldozed the fever trees on the Mkuze floodplain in KwaZulu Natal so that he could plant bananas. When the river came down in flood, as it did every year, the farmer claimed flood damage from the local government – many of whom were his personal friends. Jane was an outstanding environmental investigative journalist and true to her style she went after the farmer, raising the issue of the damage that he was doing to the ecosystem with his illegal practices. Jane's courage and determination to challenge environmental issues was the catalyst which resulted in the creation of a new wildlife area in KwaZulu-Natal.

Soon after Jane's report was published, she was at a wildlife conference listening to John telling the world how things worked. Journalists liked John because he was so outspoken. He was a master of the sound-bite and frequently came up with a phrase that spoke the proverbial thousand words. Jane jammed the microphone under his nose asking him if he was not prostituting the wilderness with safari for profit. He gave good value in his reply. During the interview John suggested that she came to see the Londolozi model for herself. I am sure that John's motivation for the invitation was not only to do with conservation.

Whatever the motivation, Jane passed the Londolozi story on to a handful of people in Durban. In particular, she talked to Trevor Coppen who had developed Sodwana Lodge on the Maputaland coast, and was

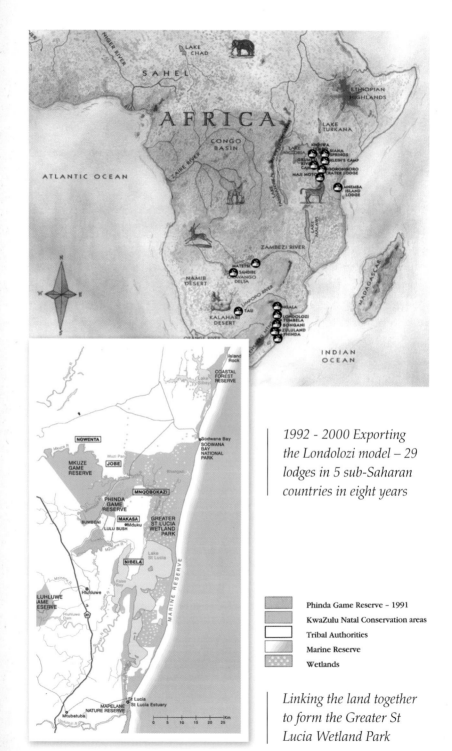

1992 - 2000 Exporting the Londolozi model – 29 lodges in 5 sub-Saharan countries in eight years

Linking the land together to form the Greater St Lucia Wetland Park

one of the moving spirits behind the idea of acquiring land that would link Sodwana, Mkuze and St Lucia together in one vast wilderness reserve. Trevor first made contact with Kevin Leo-Smith, an agricultural estate agent in Pietermaritzburg, who would know how to quietly go about getting options over farms and consolidating an area large enough to form a game reserve. Through Jane they hooked up with Alan Bernstein who had financial expertise in raising development capital and who had identified many of South Africa's dormant assets, such as airports, roads, national and provincial parks as having huge potential for tourism in the new South Africa.

Next, they made contact with the London Zoological Society and asked them to come to South Africa to see if they could endorse the project. Jane also suggested to Trevor that they should visit John Varty at Londolozi and ask him to give a talk to the London Zoological Society on his model and on what would be possible in the KwaZulu/Maputaland area.

This was exactly what we were looking for – a chance to replicate the model in a new location, and even to spread the Londolozi concept across Africa. John invited them to come to Londolozi. But, surprise, surprise, when the party rolled up, he had malaria.

I knew nothing of what was going on or what amazing tale John had woven to entice Jane to come to Londolozi. Shan and I had been busy upgrading our camps and raising Londolozi's facilities to meet Relais standards. I vaguely knew of Jane. She had written something about us in a Natal newspaper. John came staggering up to me, saying that he had to give a talk to some guys who were arriving that day. 'They want to build a game reserve like Londolozi in Zululand. You go and tell them how to do it,' he told me as he collapsed back onto his bed. So I went in my smartest torn-and-worn khaki clothes and gave this group of complete strangers the Londolozi story.

Soon after that Kevin Leo-Smith, Trevor Coppen, Alan Bernstein and I had serious discussions on the possibility of opening up some of the magical wilderness on the Maputaland coastal plain. Alan Bernstein quickly latched on to what I was talking about. He was a highly intelligent guy and a good listener and was the first to comment, 'I like your ideas. I know how to raise money.' And at great speed he gave me a heap of financial gobbledegook and talked numbers that were way beyond anything I had ever thought of.

He told me he could raise R50 million. No trouble! He was a very charismatic guy and I was intrigued. Conservation needed real funding – selling T-shirts to save rhinos was not the answer.

So I turned to Alan and said, 'Let's not complicate things. If you buy buggered-up agricultural farms and consolidate them into a large reserve, I'll put it under wildlife. Then the land value will escalate and the whole area will become more valuable. I've seen it all before at Londolozi. You raise the money. I'll run the reserve. I can replicate our model anywhere. And it will make money.'

I was super-confident and believed my own press. For 20 years, since its inception in the 1970s, Londolozi had been our fiefdom. I had all the answers. But, oh how much I still had to learn!

My brief introduction to the Maputaland coastal plain to the south of Mozambique had captured my imagination and my attention. There had once been so much beauty in this part of the world: the myriad of wetlands and waterways, the pristine beaches, the coral reefs and rocky pools, the forests of fig and fever trees, the unique sand forests and tall Kosi palms combined to create an exceptional background for safari adventures. What was of particular interest to me was that it had once been a truly magnificent wildlife habitat. Then, in the 19th century the elephants and rhinoceros were devastated by hunters.

Worse was to come when parcels of land were 'given' to ex-servicemen returning from the 1914-1918 War. Few of these men had any experience in farming and their priority was to eliminate the game which they believed carried the disease known as nagana, which was killing their cattle. The killing of wildlife over two decades culminated in a massive drive in the 1940s when almost everything that moved was shot. Apart from white rhino, which were close to extinction and were protected, only a few species survived the destruction. And then they found that the killing had done nothing to affect the tsetse fly – and by extension – the nagana.

It was not until 1946 that further research identified the tsetse fly as the culprit. Thereafter DDT spraying of the breeding areas of the tsetse fly began and the cattle disease was controlled.

At the end of the killing frenzy there were virtually no predators and not all that many antelope species left in the remnant parks set aside for wildlife. But there were hippo in the rivers, a nucleus of white rhinoceros that under Ian Player's guiding hand was saved from extinction, and a spectacular variety of bird species. Later on, under the apartheid homeland system, a sea of poverty rose out of the sandy plain, further destroying the biodiversity of the region.

Now, a new era was about to begin. It seemed likely that Nelson Mandela would be the next president. His primary responsibility would be sociological – he needed to be seen to be levelling the playing fields. It was clear to us that wildlife funding would be low on his list of priorities. However, having met Mandela, I knew that he recognised the political advantages of having a developing safari industry in South Africa. He had told me that if we demonstrated that our endeavours brought benefits to the people, when the ANC came to power we could expect his full support.

We wanted to be ready to participate in the economic benefits of being back on the world stage. We had identified dormant opportunities that had arisen out of our past history – land never intended for farming had been farmed to oblivion; wildlife had disappeared, leaving an empty silent wilderness; people had been moved from green hills onto coastal land unsuitable for farming; dams had been built for the purpose of irrigating crops to please minority farming groups and with no thought of the effect on the land downstream; and military roads and runways of high standard had been built for the nation's security, but would serve a tourism industry equally well. There was clearly a strength in using the Londolozi model: our self-motivated workforce and our community involvement were way ahead of their time and could be of significant benefit to this new region.

Alan took me to look at the farms that were to become Phinda. It was a hellhole. I had come from the Sabi Sand where a 55 000-hectare consolidated game reserve had been founded in 1954 and where we had spent time and money over two decades caring for the reserve. Phinda had a public road running right through the middle of it. It was criss-crossed with fences and power lines and was littered with the debris of failed agriculture. What was left for us was a legacy of inappropriate land-use practices propped up by government ideologies that had allowed an organisation called the Land Bank to give loans to farmers who all too frequently went against nature and failed. From the outset there was never any chance that those loans would be repaid.

I took in the scene, the rusted fences and machinery and habitat invaded by dense alien bush after cattle had overgrazed the land.

Phinda - a keystone property in the creation of the greater St Lucia Wetland Park

Some fields still had sisal sprouting between ilala palms and here and there a few pineapples were ripening (our first young elephants loved them). Even portions of the unique dry sandveld forest had fallen under the blade of a bulldozer. Nothing of this once remarkable wetland was sacrosanct. Even though the soils were highly leached and saline and were so nutrient-poor that they could barely sustain a crop for more than one season, there was no doubt in my mind that it could again be a wildlife paradise.

Phinda Izilwane (Zulu words meaning 'the return of the wildlife') was a compelling vision. We were looking at a series of farms that, if consolidated, would link the Sodwana State Forest and reserves surrounding the St Lucia Estuary to the east and Mkuze Game Reserve to the west. Conservation authorities had been trying for more than 40 years to consolidate these reserves but government had been far more interested in supporting white farmers and failing land-use practices. Previously, it had had no chance of happening.

Phinda was exactly what I was looking for, a conservation development model where Londolozi could be replicated. We could take abused land and turn the clock back to when the African landscape had been pristine and we could prove that land under wildlife would have the potential to strengthen rural economies. My grandfather was one of the founders of the Sabi Sand Wildtuin. Here was an exciting opportunity for me to follow in his footsteps and create another private game reserve. Here was land damaged by cattle farming, just as the Londolozi lands had been in the 1920s. There were also impoverished rural communities that needed help and that was right on my page. Another incentive was that even in those early days there was talk of St Lucia being designated a World Heritage Site. Although we would be on the other side of the fence, when it did happen it was bound to affect our land value.

On the eastern shore of the St Lucia estuary there was a major conflict going on between the conservationists and the industrialists who wanted to mine the sand dunes using water from the estuary for a titanium mining venture. The salinity level of the lake had already risen to a concentration that would kill off many species. The Natal Parks Board was prepared to fight tooth and nail to prevent any more damage to this magnificent area and promised that the safari industry would provide just as many jobs for far longer than the years spent recovering the heavy metals.

Phinda had potential. Only a century earlier it had been an interconnected wonder-wetland. I believed that it could be restored if we took the good points and built on them. We were to discover that the area contained seven different ecosystems and could support a wonderful biodiversity of life. We had frogs everywhere. The birdlife was magnificent. And the insects were spectacular. All we would need to give it commercial value in tourism would be to reintroduce the big five, increase the diversity of antelope and bring in a few other animals like wild dogs and giraffe. We had at our fingertips a vast reservoir of technology which we could apply to relocate animals. We would also need to install infrastructure over the 15 000 hectare area: electrified fences, tracks, small dams, telephone lines, water supply and power cables. Finally we would build lodges of world class standards for international visitors.

Apart from a belief in my ability to fix the land and the wildlife, the wise counsel of Ken Tinley was available to us. He had grown up in

Natal and had spent the early days of his career working with Ian Player as a game ranger for the Natal Parks Board. More than 10 years earlier, when Ken was showing us how to repair Londolozi's land, he had invited us to his brother's home, ironically on the farm Zulu Nyala which eventually formed the southern sector of Phinda. Charles Tinley had developed a wildlife, multi-use model on the land several years earlier. He was convinced that, with a little care, the nyala and impala herds could be built up in the region.

Looking across the derelict farmland on the Maputaland coastal plain, I knew enough to believe that our dream was possible. But for others it might have been hard to see that there was any chance of restoring the devastated landscape into another Londolozi and that it could become a desirable tourism destination. At that stage, to my mind, we had only one problem: it needed to be bigger if it was to move from being just another game ranch in Zululand into a fully interpretive game reserve experience.

So I told my new friends: 'Get hold of more land, tear out all the internal fences, put one perimeter fence around all the land and work on linking up with the state reserves.'

At that stage Kevin Leo-Smith and Trevor Coppen had secured options over only 8 000 hectares to the south of the Mkuze River. Tinley's advice to me was to establish the park wetland to wetland, linking the Mzinene River in the south to the Mkuze floodplains in the north. It would mean acquiring more land. In any case, the piece we had was far too small to be a viable game reserve and there were still some holes that needed to be filled.

Despite the enormity of the task, we were undaunted and we poured our energies into making Phinda happen. Failure was not on our agenda.

Photograph: Richard du Toit

YOU RAISE IT. I'LL RUN IT.

We thought that all we had to do to get our project off the drawing board was to find the mere R60 million to create the new reserve and convince our rural neighbours of the merit of our conservation development project. Alan Bernstein saw no difficulty in raising the funds and I went along on what I thought would be a really worthwhile venture for this much abused planet.

Our first port of call was Gencor – one of the big mining and financial institutions based in Johannesburg. The intrepid young Al and young Dave set off. I had given my conservation story so many times to politicians, businessmen and fireside guests that my task was easy. For me the financial story from Alan was spellbinding. And so was the reply: 'Okay, boys. You've got R100 million in principle. You, the promoters, can have 20 per cent. We're floating a safari division in Gencor. Just one thing, we'll need to get this ratified at our board meeting on Monday. This should be no problem.'

After one meeting Dave and Al were R20 million richer. All we had to do was build Phinda into a paradise. That night we popped the champagne. But our celebration proved to be premature.

Something went wrong at the board meeting. Word came down that what had been said on Friday was not the case on Monday. Our timing was all wrong: you cannot delist a non-core subsidiary and launch another non-core operation during the same board meeting. The project was vetoed. It was a devastating blow. Phinda died before it was born. It was my first lesson in corporate behaviour: often, all is not what it seems.

I was to learn that raising R100 million takes more than just one presentation and brings with it many hidden demands. Almost before our journey began we had hit our first 'oops'. More were to follow, along the way.

We decided we needed to take a step back and rethink. So Alan went fishing at Sodwana on the Maputaland coast. The captain of the Western Province big game fishing team was also there. Alan struck up a conversation with him, telling him about our grand idea of building a reserve, wetland to wetland, and being the catalyst for the formation of a Greater St Lucia Wetland Park that would rival the Kruger National Park. Alan was never one to undersell our position. He had an indomitable spirit and was unbowed by the setback of the day before.

The Western Province big game fishing team captain was Koos Jonker, a man who was full of his own creative funding ideas and managing director of a company called Masterbond. He was enthusiastic about our project and expressed a willingness to support us financially. History has proved that this support gave Phinda life. However, a few months later Masterbond collapsed. At the time it was the largest financial drama to unfold in South Africa. With its demise many pensioners and investors lost their entire savings and Phinda was nearly dragged under in the ensuing mess.

The short-term debenture debt provided by Masterbond was, at that stage, central to our financial strategy. But it was also an entirely inappropriate financial instrument to fund a long-term project. What we did not know at the time was that we were being supported by a bank that was a ticking time bomb. Nonetheless we had access to funding of R35 million and Phinda was being assembled.

Soon after that I met Trevor Shaw at one of those functions where you wear a name tag. Trevor marched up to me and, recognising my name, introduced himself by saying, 'You're the guy I'm looking for. I'm building the best lodge in the world. It's called Zulu Nyala. I'm no good at looking after guests. They give me too much of a hard time. You must come and run my lodge for me.'

Despite the fact that I've yet to meet a lodge owner who has not 'built the best lodge in the world', I could hardly contain my excitement. I knew that Trevor Shaw owned the farm which was the ecological link to take Phinda south onto the Mzinene River.

So I said, 'I won't run your lodge for you but I'll buy your land.'

I had caught the fever from Alan and a few extra million here and there was 'nothing', given the grand idea that we were developing. I had nearly raised R100 million from Gencor and I had just raised R35 million from Masterbond. This bush boy had been seduced by these big numbers and thought it was easy.

So I asked him: 'How much?'

'Okay, if you've got R12 million in your pocket, I might talk.'

'We'll get back to you,' I replied.

So I went back to Alan. I told him that if we bought Shaw's property we could link wetland to wetland – from the Mkuze River in the north to the Mzinene River in the south. This would make Phinda credible as a reserve and no longer a game ranch. I was determined that we would achieve this goal.

Fences could now come down and the spark was ignited for the creation of a huge Greater St Lucia Wetland Park, which would stretch all the way from the St Lucia Estuary, north to the Mkuze River and inland to include Mkuze Game Reserve and Phinda.

For now we needed more money to buy Shaw's land. So we went back to Koos Jonker. He revalued our property and increased our loan facility to R60 million, handing us a cheque for R12 million as we left the building. This was real money for real conservation development. It was a new experience for me and it was thrilling. We then called Shaw to ask him where we should deposit the money.

After some further haggling we acquired the southern section of Phinda which included the north bank of the Mzinene River. The half-built lodge on top of the hill was not at all in keeping with our style of low-impact eco-lodges that we hid from view or blended into the landscape. But the half-built concrete 'monsterpiece' on the top of the hill, had a splendid view overlooking the northern end of Lake St Lucia and all the way to the dunes of the Indian Ocean. We had a 14 000-hectare chunk of land with huge potential – even if there were many problems that needed to be put right. This was what conservation development was all about: using the energy that money provides, if wisely directed, to bring more land and complete ecosystems in Africa under wildlife.

In 1991 the construction of 120 kilometres of game fence construction began. Les Carlisle, the moving spirit in creating a wilderness wonderland at Phinda, was appointed land manager. The major restocking exercise he led turned out to be the largest relocation of wildlife ever undertaken in South Africa at that time. Then we started to repair the massive erosion and encroachment caused by cattle ranching activities and we removed the rusted farm debris. Very soon we had elephants, lions, cheetah and white rhino. Les even packed a python into his lunch box and carried it back to Phinda for release. It was quite a story on its own.

From the Gencor presentation to the creation of Phinda was, in reality, no more than nine months of flat-out work. Things happened so fast that we hardly had time to catch our breath. While Alan was busy sorting out the next step in the financing of the Phinda development, Howard Geech, a friend of Alan's who was so enthralled by our conservation development model that he threw up a promising career in Anglo American to join us, attended a conference on dune mining in the St Lucia area. He is highly articulate and knowledgeable on wildlife matters and with his Anglo American management training skills, he gave the mine developers a lot to think about in a rousing speech at the Richard's Bay conference.

'Do you think you should be mining non-unique minerals on unique land?' he asked.

He'd caught the disease from Dave and Al and proceeded to tell the assembled group that we could develop a safari industry from Maputo to Hluhluwe – that we wanted to join forces with them and take down the fences between wildlife and wildlife. He ended his talk with the comment, 'You can stop mining the beach, safari is the future for this region.'

During the conference Howard ran into Dr Robbie Robinson who had just been appointed chief executive of South African National Parks. Robinson told him that he had a problem. Hans Hohuisen had donated the 14 000-hectare Ngala Game Reserve adjacent to the Kruger National Park to the WWF and South Africa National Parks Trust of which Robbie was a trustee. Valued at R80 million, it was the largest donation ever made to the WWF. But the Ngala lodge operations were costing South African National Parks R250 000 a month. Robbie Robinson was quick to take the decision that they should not be in the luxury safari lodge business. He told Howard, 'I've got a lodge I want you to run. I want you guys to make it like Londolozi.'

Howard Geech reported back, telling me that the CEO of the National Parks wanted to see me.

My instinctive reply was, 'Just do me a favour: don't waste your time and mine. I've been at variance with the National Parks since 1970 when I got thrown out because I wanted to make money out of wildlife and because of our ideas on community, tourism and land management. It hasn't helped our relationship that Nelson Mandela recently endorsed Londolozi as a model for future conservation in South Africa.'

'No,' I told Howard. 'We've got better things to do. I'm much too busy.'

But Howard persisted. 'Look, come with me to see Robinson. Just once.'

Reluctantly, I agreed and the following Saturday morning drove out to Pretoria and pressed the buzzer at the National Parks Board's front door.

A guy came strolling out in track suit and takkies. I said rather aggressively, 'We're here to see Dr Robinson.' His reply, 'That's me,' took me by surprise. No epaulettes, no berets, no smart uniform.

'You're Dr Robinson?' I said, hardly disguising my astonishment. He nodded. 'Well, we're here to see you,' I continued in an aggressive tone.

I made no bones about it. I was expecting the same old rhetoric from the hard-line Park's Board officials wedded to the management master plan which excluded surrounding communities and kept the park for the exclusive few.

Robinson said, 'Come and have some tea at my house.'

So we walked down the road and I had a few moments to think, 'This isn't a Parks Board approach. No official office. No defensive hackles out! This guy is different.'

Before we sat down I asked him, 'Have you ever heard of a guy called Ken Tinley?'

His reply took the wind out of my sails. 'Ken Tinley,' he said, 'he's the greatest ecologist in South Africa. That's the guy we should have followed years ago. He's really got something.' We became instant friends.

I had spent 15 years selling Ken Tinley and everyone had told me he was too radical. Robinson was right on my page. We agreed on everything. Along the way I learn that Robbie was from Southern Parks in the Cape. It was unheard of that a forward-thinking man from the Cape should be given the all-powerful CEO position of the National Parks Board in Pretoria – a job that had previously been reserved for the hard-liners.

The meeting set in motion the negotiations for the rights to a long-term lease over Ngala and the surrounding property. It was hugely forward thinking for the National Park and hugely advantageous for us. In fact, it was the first ever commercial partnership between National Parks, an NGO (the WWF), and the private sector. We were able to secure the use-rights of an R80 million asset for 20 years. This was a test case for unlocking the potential of the National Parks' underutilised assets. More recently, concessions for private enterprise have been opened up within reserves such as the Kruger National Park.

Not long after this I flew to Stellenbosch to meet with Robbie Robinson and Frans Stroebel who represented the South African

Nature Foundation founded by Dr Anton Rupert, which after 1994 became WWF South Africa. The documents for a 10-year lease of Ngala, with the option to renew for a further decade, had been prepared and were tabled in front of us.

Just before signing Robbie paused and asked: 'Is jy besig om bankrot te speel.' (Are you about to go bankrupt?)

I did not hesitate and replied: 'Probably, but if you sign that piece of paper we won't!'

He knew that Conservation Corporation Africa and Phinda were precariously hanging in the balance but, nevertheless, he signed, handed me the document and wished me good luck. It was a bold and visionary move on the part of an individual in a position of authority. It was certainly a key point in the creation of Phinda and the success of CCAfrica.

We had got further than I could ever have dreamed possible in that first year. We had exported our model into Maputaland and were hard at work bringing land back to life and we had landed the first ever private concession within the Kruger National Park. Surely, with time, our conservation and human resource model would influence the government-controlled National Parks policy. The success of the Londolozi model, after all, was there for everyone to see.

Our major problem now was to secure funds for our development. We had started to realise that raising money was not an easy process. It would take time and effort and more than our fair share of luck. At least we had two great properties with huge potential and we appreciated just how much work it would take to get both up to the high standards we had set ourselves. Phinda needed a magic wand to bring the wildlife back. Ngala needed imagination to turn an ugly duckling into a swan.

Before we went into the next phase of development, we decided to take a break and get to know each other. Howard Geech, Alan and I decided to go canoeing on the Zambezi – about 40 kilometres upstream from the Victoria Falls. We started our canoeing safari, clad, as you would expect, in our bathing shorts and bright yellow life jackets – the remainder of our equipment was to be transported down river where we would arrive later that day.

Some way downstream our guide, a typical Rambo-Zimbo boytjie, advised the team that we were approaching the famous Katombora Rapids.

'Girls go down the right channel. Boys go down the left,' he said. 'Which way do you want to go?'

Of course, the bullet-proof brigade had no hesitation in shouting: 'Left!'

But we soon discovered that the only navigable channel down the left side was blocked by a fallen tree and within seconds we were at the mercy of this mighty river. There was nowhere to go. And there was no reverse gear. In a split second we were sideways on, jammed by the current against rocks and had white water pouring over us. We were in real trouble and were lucky to be able to extricate ourselves from our canoe, which had turned turtle. We rode down the rapids in our life jackets, miraculously avoiding a head-on collision with the many rocky outcrops that punctuated the rapids. One canoe snapped in two. One of the guys in it went missing for several hours: we thought he had drowned. It was to be the first of many close shaves with Africa. Eventually, bedraggled and shocked, we pulled ourselves out onto the north bank of the river, altogether forgetting about the Zambezi crocodiles and the fact that we had now illegally crossed an international boundary. More was to come.

As we began to reorganise ourselves, an armed man in uniform approached us. I greeted the Zambian in my usual way, assuming that as we now belonged to a new democratic South Africa, all would be well. Then our Zimbabwean guide quietly told us to get into our canoes and get going quickly. But when we made our move, the attitude of the gun-wielding Zambian changed. Suddenly more armed people appeared out of the bush. Some were just kids brandishing handguns which were fully cocked and pretty menacing. We found ourselves staring into the barrels of automatic weapons. We were then marched at gunpoint through the bush and told: 'You have no passports, you are illegal in this country. You know, recently Mr Mugabe gave an instruction to his army to shoot on sight any Zambians who arrived illegally in Zimbabwe. What should we do with you?' We were in a worrying situation. The young heroes from South Africa were taking yet another lesson from the great African teacher.

The previous night we had had animated discussions around the campfire about the folly of international boundaries.

'Africa's wildlife once walked across the whole African continent,' I said. 'How is it that we are so arrogant that we impose boundaries which

*Discussing the removal of fences on the beach at Sodwana with
Dr Robinson, CEO SANParks, 1994*

are not related to the ecology of a region?' I finished my lecture with the comment, 'We share the river. It belongs to us all.'

Our guide tried this line on the very important Zambian official who was deciding our fate. But he did not agree with our expansive view and we were unceremoniously bundled into a police van, fate and destination unknown, still dressed in our life jackets, swimming shorts and with one flip-flop between us which – for some inexplicable reason – had stayed attached to Alan's right foot. And, of course, we had no passports.

One place you do not want to be on a Friday afternoon in Zambia is in the back of a police van. The first priority of the driver is to get home quickly. The second priority is a warm alcoholic beverage that will make the journey less tedious. So the speedometer climbed rapidly as we zigzagged our way, dodging potholes at about 120 km an hour. From the rear of our truck we saw a military vehicle approaching, which – with the driver in the same state of mind as ours – attempted to overtake us on the narrow road. Picture the scene: two worn-out government vehicles, two drivers racing home, lots of warm beer, and guns. Just as the army vehicle got alongside, our driver swerved to avoid a pothole. Both vehicles nearly overturned. But, by the grace of God, we arrived in Livingstone in one piece.

By that time the Livingstone border post was closed and, still clad only in our bathing shorts (and still with one flip-flop), we were handed over to the head of immigration. But this was the wrong place: we were told that as the border post was closed we had to go to Internal Affairs. Here we told our story for the umpteenth time. For the first time the mood lightened.

'It appears that you have suffered from a misadventure,' the official said.

'Yes, sir, we have indeed,' I replied.

'And furthermore,' he continued, partly for the benefit of the other officials and definitely with a twinkle in his eye, 'if you were coming to invade our country, I hardly think you would come dressed like that,' referring to our severely torn lifejackets, shorts and the single flip-flop which seemed to stay with us.

Nervous laughter grew into uncontrolled mirth as at ten o'clock at night he launched on the junior officials who had gathered along the way. With the theatrical flair that is so wonderfully and truly African, he said, 'I am sick up and fed of this bloody nonsense. Can't you see these men are on holiday? Why do you not leave them to continue their canoe safari? You make unnecessary trouble for all of us. Take them to the Mosi-o-Tunya Hotel where they will be my guests for the night.'

So, from having guns stuck in our ribs, we were guests of the state in the best hotel in Livingstone. We had a four-course meal – still dressed only in our bathing shorts – and slept well. But our problems were not over yet.

When the border post opened in the morning, we were no longer the responsibility of our new friend in Internal Affairs. Once again we fell under the jurisdiction of the very men he had crapped on! We were re-arrested. Fortunately our people had heard via the bush telegraph that a bunch of tourists were under arrest in Livingstone and they had come over with our passports. So with much relief we were eventually allowed to leave Zambia.

The irony of this was that three years later, we would own the concession on the Zimbabwean side of the Zambezi right opposite the Katombora Rapids.

So much for our relaxing weekend!

*Capturing elephants
in Kruger Park
destined for Phinda*

NEW JUNGLE. NEW RULES

With Masterbond's R60 million short-term loan finance facility and two magnificent sites we were on our way. But our priority was to convert short-term debt into long-term equity. I was aware of the financial pressures we faced – that long-term conservation development cannot be funded by short-term debt. Added to that, we were soon to discover that Hambros Bank, our potential backer in London, was not confident about Masterbond's future. But that was Alan's department. I was in lodge-building mode and was up to my eyes in every aspect of construction of the 40-bed Phinda Mountain Lodge. At the same time we were starting our plans to refurbish Ngala.

Les Carlisle was going at full steam relocating animals into Phinda and trying to bring back a herd of elephants – recently relocated from the Kruger Park – that had torn down our electric fence and were on their way to the Hluhluwe supermarket. Les recovered a dozen elephants on a cold, moonless night. It was a remarkable feat involving private enterprise and the KwaZulu-Natal Parks Board, and once again showed that the people on the ground could work together with great success.

Then Alan arrived on site. He needed me in London. Jan Newman of Hambros Bank had come to South Africa to find out whether, despite the fact that the ANC was still calling for sanctions, the time was right for Hambros to again enter the South African merchant banking market. He suggested to Alan that fund-raising for CCAfrica could be their first project.

Under Alan's instruction I headed for the top men's designer clothing store in Hyde Park, Johannesburg to purchase my 'battle fatigues'. Two Hermes ties, two Hugo Boss suits, two Etienne Agner shirts, one Etienne Agner leather belt and one pair of Church shoes – black. This was standard attire for the London banking scene. 'No brown or grey shoes, please.'

My response to this was: 'Hell! Alan, with this kind of money I could have bought a gold-plated Land Rover!'

However, I donned my suit and my Hermes tie and went to London to tell our amazing South African investment story to the deputy chairman of Hambros Bank. We were talking rights issues, which they would

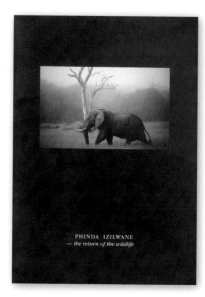

PHINDA IZILWANE
— *the return of the wildlife*

This announcement appears as a matter of record only

R59 million

Raised by
international private placement

for

THE CONSERVATION CORPORATION

South Africa's largest private conservation project

The undersigned acted as financial adviser to
The Conservation Corporation and sponsored
and underwrote the fund raising

🦁 HAMBROS BANK LIMITED

41 Tower Hill, London EC3N 4HA

Member of the SFA and IMRO

*Bringing
a business
approach to
conservation
– real money
for real
conservation
– 1992*

underwrite to replace the short-term debt finance that we had with Masterbond. I was a bit out of my depth. In all the years I had spent building up Londolozi, I never looked further for funding than extending an overdraft facility – which admittedly sometimes went beyond the happy equilibrium of our bank manager. What we did understand was that if you took his money and you did not pay it back, he took your farm. It was clear-cut. All the fancy new financial terminology was dazzling. I was later to learn that, despite jetting around the world in my Church shoes (which gave me blisters), the name of the game is the same: if you want your business to be a success, more cash must come in than goes out, no matter what shoes you wear.

So there I was at 41 Tower Hill, London, uncomfortably dressed to the nines. I got to the Hambros office at eight o'clock – which is like midday in the safari business. An hour later the first banker pitched up. Around ten o'clock more bankers came dribbling in. I'd been sitting there for two hours when I finally told someone that I was there to see Mr Jonathan Klein who had been appointed to handle our business.

I was told, in a broad Cockney accent, 'Mr Klein! 'E'll not be 'ere today, Sir. England is playing Australia. You'll find 'im at Lord's.'

I discovered that Jonathan Klein had it written into his contract that when the England cricket team were playing at Lord's he could take the day off. The first day of my international fund-raising effort was spent twiddling my thumbs in some very expensive offices overlooking Tower Bridge.

The next day we met Jonathan Klein, who turned out to be a highly entertaining character and extremely astute. He had with him a young assistant who was built in the same mould, articulate, bright and with a truly wicked sense of humour. When I first met Mark Getty, his surname meant nothing to me. I was only later to learn that he was heir apparent to the Getty fortune. I also had no idea of the important part he would play in our future affairs. Our fund-raising safari with Jonathan and Mark was punctuated with entertainment and the kind of fun that will live with me for a lifetime. I'm eternally grateful for what I learnt from these two bright people although, in retrospect, I would have a thing or two to say about the financial structures they created.

Jon, originally from South Africa, saw our investment as a chance to contribute to the newly emerging democracy. He and Mark interested themselves in our project at once.

They told us: 'You've got eight minutes to talk to our boss, Christopher Sporborg. He's deputy chairman of Hambros. This is your opportunity. If he says yes, Hambros will underwrite your project and we'll have permission to take you on a fund-raising road show. If he says no, the project will be dead and you can go back to the bush.'

Alan and I delivered our maiden investor presentation – modified from the Gencor/Masterbond sales pitch – reminding Mark and Jon that it was old hat. We had done it all before. From our point of view we gave a command performance. It was nothing short of brilliant and 50 minutes later we bade Mr Sporborg goodbye, expecting Jon and Mark to congratulate us on our superb effort. We were totally taken aback at the abuse that was hurled at us. Jon and Mark agreed that it was undoubtedly the worst presentation they had ever heard.

Jon was scathing, 'I said you had eight minutes. You took 50! You were too garrulous. In this game, if you are asked a bloody question, answer it. Don't give your life history.'

We thought we would be crucified. However, to Jon's and Mark's amazement, Christopher liked our enthusiasm and gave the project Hambros backing.

Right from the start we were on a hiding to nothing. I had bankers in smart suits in London telling me that we would raise R35 million to replace the initial Masterbond funds and if we could produce a 33 per cent internal rate of return within three years, management could claw back an equity share in the business. I was more than a little taken aback. Even the bush boy can work out that a 33 per cent return on R35 million within three years is not feasible on a grassroots safari lodge investment in the middle of war-torn KwaZulu-Natal where there is no big game, no scheduled air service and international tourists have never heard of the place. Not least of all, when I last looked, we needed R60 million.

We never caught up. For a decade we were always short of funds. And we never had a look-in when it came to management equity participation.

It's hard to believe just how far from reality the investment funding was. The bulk of the money we raised had been taken up buying the Phinda farms, restoring the land and bringing in the wildlife. Certainly, our half-built lodge, designed for 40 beds, was not going to bring in enough money. But my job was not the financial side of the deal and what we needed was to raise money to replace the Masterbond short-term debt. There was a rumour that Masterbond was folding. We needed another line of credit and we needed equity. Suddenly, everything we had done so far was at risk. Alan told me: 'We have to find other funders soon or Phinda will be dead!'

Although my instincts told me otherwise, I went along with the proposal. To me, money is a means to an end and not the end in itself. I wanted to advance green frontiers and prove the case for conservation development. Expediency and compromise were to live with me for a decade. Failure to trust my gut was my major downfall and I learnt a hard lesson.

'What we need,' announced Jon Klein, 'is a prospectus.'

'Right,' I said, but I'm thinking: 'What's a prospectus?'

Later on I found out that it was like a marketing brochure but in financial 'speak'. I could relate to that. So for weeks, Al and I, with a team of lawyers and bankers, authored an investor prospectus. The detail was painstaking. The costs were horrendous. And I couldn't see how this was going to help me get the job done in Africa. All I knew was that every dollar or pound sterling that I spent on that stuff needed to be paid back by frying eggs for happy guests at Phinda. I knew this was not going to be an easy job and I grew increasingly worried and frustrated about the process.

As soon as the paperwork was done, we hit the road. Our objective was to raise R39 million and convert the short-term debenture funding provided by Masterbond into long-term equity. We made more than 200 presentations in the months we travelled in America, Europe and the UK. Singing our song was uphill all the way. And we got nowhere!

We addressed corporate equity investors and fund managers of varying descriptions. Look at it from their point of view. Sitting in the comfort of their London, New York, Boston and Dublin offices, listening to wide-eyed Africans delivering a presentation that went something like this: 'Yes, we've identified some bankrupt farms in northern KwaZulu-Natal. The Zulus live there. Yes, there were farmers there once – but all the farmers went bankrupt and left. No, that does not mean that we cannot succeed. You see it's a floodplain and that's not good for farming. Yes, it gets flooded every year but that's good for wildlife. The Zulus? Well, they are planning to attack the ANC supporters. But we don't think this will develop into a civil war. Yes, they are the same warlike people who beat the shit out of the British. But that was in 1879. Things are different now. I beg your pardon, you say that there are more violent deaths in Zululand than in any other part of the world? Well, we don't think that state of affairs will last long – not after our first democratic elections. When will that be? Well, we don't know but President de Klerk and Mr Mandela are working on it. We'll get on with the job of fixing up the farms. We'll take down the rusty fences and put up a new one. Then we'll stock the whole place with wildlife. Game viewing? Well, right now you can't see a thing – just a few nyala. And plenty of frogs. But we're making plans. We'll get elephants, lions, cheetah and rhinoceros. Probably leopards too. All the dangerous animals. Then we'll take out the bush encroachment. I beg your pardon? That came because the farmers cleared the natural bush. Yes, it will take time. How long? Possibly years. But in the end, we'll have a superb safari destination.'

We were slick. We thought we had all the answers. But we were not getting to first base. One Asian executive commented, 'Yes, a very interesting presentation. So tell me, who gets the first dollar? Is it the lion? Or is it the investor?' That floored us.

The people we went to see were seriously big fund managers. But they were managing other people's money and were obliged to stay in the safety zone. We had no chance. What we needed was a champion of the project – an independent investor who would attract other investors. We thought we would never find one. We were singularly unsuccessful in Europe, the United Kingdom and Ireland. Only Hambros was sympathetic. Then Mark Getty suggested that we went to see one of his family investment advisers. If he gave his stamp of approval Mark said he would take the proposition to the rest of his family. Although I had not realised it then, Mark was the champion we needed. In every respect he understood our aims and objectives and believed that we would succeed. He also had access to one of the largest family fortunes in the world. He was our only glimmer of hope in an otherwise unsuccessful fund-raising road show.

In the meantime we returned home, visibly despondent. At the same time there was a lot going on at Phinda. We had more than 400 workers on site and they were motoring. Then I got a summons from Mark: 'Come to New York.' By this time we had a fair idea of the support that Mark could bring to us.

Once again I exchanged my bush clothes for my 'asking-for-money' outfit, joined Alan in Johannesburg and set off for London. We immediately transferred onto the Concorde (in those days a BA special if you flew business class to London) and arrived in New York ready to meet for a before-dinner glass of champagne at the Getty adviser's apartment on Fifth Avenue.

But I had no time to catch up with myself. I was hungry, thirsty and exhausted. So was Alan. Without thinking, I had three glasses of champagne in quick succession and was suddenly legless and slurring my words. Jon Klein saw what was going on and shielded me from view, while Mark bundled me into a cab. We had a 20-minute drive from the apartment to a very fancy restaurant in New York. I catnapped in the cab and when we arrived at the restaurant, Mark told me that I couldn't let him down. He'd gone out on a limb for this meeting. 'Varty, this is a respected adviser to the family and you choose tonight to get drunk. Have you lost your marbles?'

They poured a couple of cups of black coffee down my throat while Alan Bernstein held the fort with Mr Big. Over dinner we spoke about everything else except what we'd come to discuss. I was still keeping a low profile, but was recovering slowly. Finally it was my turn to tell our fantastic story. By that time I could talk without slurring my words. I launched into it for the two-hundredth time and reached the subject of the numbers. This was my cue to hand over to Alan and I looked across the table at him. But I saw that he had run out of steam. A combination of weeks of stress and jetlag from the rapid Concorde crossing of the Atlantic had taken its toll. He had literally fallen with his face in his dessert plate! We had by now made so many investor presentations that I was able to give the financial side of the story parrot-fashion, using all the big words that only a few months earlier were a foreign language to me. So I made a start while Mark belted Alan across the knees to wake him up. Without missing a beat, he wiped the cream off his face and launched into his story. Afterwards we laughed until we cried, and Mark had a few choice things to say to both of us.

From that presentation we went west to San Francisco. A meeting was set up with Judge Bill Newsom who was a great and trusted friend of Gordon Getty's, a trustee of three of the four Getty Trusts and a serious conservationist. He could be described as the family 'Mr Fixit', a highly intelligent, witty guy with a huge heart. Once again we told our story and I gathered that he was checking us out. We still had no idea that the Getty family would even consider taking a major stake in our business. Such is life in the investment world of smokescreens and mirrors. But we were getting the idea.

Soon after that we were back in New York and on the 40th floor of the Ford Foundation. We were invited to lunch with John English, the head of the Ford Foundation investment arm. There's no way that we would have got past the janitor at the front door without the Getty influence. They opened doors for us.

Once again I gave our pitch but I felt the need to embellish my story. Through the few weeks of our road show, the bush boy had become a world authority on money management and investment in various sectors. Coming from South Africa, gold had become my speciality. I brought my presentation to a grand finale with the comment: 'This investment's better than gold.'

John English was a polite and unassuming gentleman. He invited us to lunch but declined the investment. As we headed down in the lift, Mark suggested that I should drop the line about gold. 'After all, the Ford Foundation's investment arm has about 20 per cent of its $6 billion portfolio invested in gold stocks.'

The day before, on Alan's suggestion and because of the rumour in the marketplace that had been picked up by Jon Klein, we asked Shan, who was holding the fort in Johannesburg, to phone Koos Jonker at Masterbond and advise him that she was faxing a request for a further draw-down of R3 million on the Phinda building project. He confirmed that it was fine. She immediately faxed him the routine request and the very next morning received a faxed reply from Masterbond: 'Expect no further cash advances'.

Geoff Ash, our project manager at Phinda, was calling for the next draw-down. Shan needed R3 million the next day and asked us: 'What do I do? A 400-strong construction team is waiting to be paid.' Things were getting tense in Zululand.

Because Jon Klein and Mark Getty had correctly read that Masterbond might go bust, they had put an alternative line of credit in place that kept us going. But we were desperately short of funds to complete the building of Mountain Lodge and continue with putting up fences and the relocation of wildlife, which was well under way at Phinda. But Phinda was technically owned by the creditors of Masterbond and was on the verge of falling into a cauldron of legal action that was to churn around for a decade. Masterbond was out and the new investors were not in. We were walking on a tightrope.

But we were not altogether desperate. A ray of hope appeared as Mark indicated that his family was planning a visit to Phinda, and we felt that we were close to securing the AECI Pension Fund as investors. And, of course, our alternative line of credit, although dwindling fast, was still in place.

Alan and I paid an urgent visit to the curators of Masterbond in Cape Town, intending to offer to buy the debentures off them right there and then. With Masterbond's collapse, R780 million had been lost and the investors were desperate and angry. To save Phinda we needed to get out from under the mess before the entire legal process became moribund. Furthermore, it would be embarrassing to explain to the Gettys that the core investment was already caught up in litigation even before it had opened its doors.

We arrived at the curator's office and they treated us like absolute criminals. As far as they were concerned we had Masterbond's money and they wanted our assets. We were the enemy and were told that the curator would not see us. Not before they had unravelled the situation – or acquired our land. A despondent Alan Bernstein said, 'We'd better leave.'

But my bush survival instincts came into play and I replied, 'What are you talking about? Leave now and see Phinda get lost in this mess which is not of our making?'

'Well, they say they won't see us,' he said. The Insead School of Business did not have a course on how to ambush a man in his own boardroom.

'We stay!' I told Alan. 'It's not what they say, it's what we do.' I quickly hatched a plan and we slipped past the receptionist and planted ourselves where the curator would see us when the meeting which was taking place in an adjoining office broke up. 'Come and sit right here,' I told Alan.

But he was still not on my wavelength: 'What do you think you are going to achieve by sitting?' he asked.

'Just wait,' I told him.

So we sat outside their boardroom and shot the breeze, bemoaning our fate and the unfairness of life. Eventually, at about six o'clock, the

Phinda oversubscription probed

CAPE TOWN — Because of Masterbond administrators' lack of discipline, the R43m invested by Masterbond debenture holders in northern Natal game reserve Phinda might have to be divided between more people than those on its register.

Repayment of the R43m liability has been secured by the Conservation Corporation Group, which has raised R63m on local and international markets.

Masterbond provisional curator Franz Malherbe said yesterday there was a suspicion that Masterbond administrators had duplicated the issue of debenture certificates. It was not possible to judge the

LINDA ENSOR

extent of oversubscription as the matter was still being investigated.

Curators believe that the oversubscription will not exceed 5% of the total value of the capital loan to Phinda.

Malherbe said it was possible that the names of people whose debentures were due to mature just before the Masterbond group's collapse were "illegally and unknowingly" removed from the register.

Malherbe stressed that everyone with a proper certificate would be paid whether or not they were on the register.

Picture: ANDRZEJ SAWA

BUSH BARONS ... Alan Bernstein and Dave Varty, working the corporate jungle

Conservation that pays its way

By SVEN LUNSCHE

A PASSIONATE commitment to conservation and unashamed elitism. These two characteristics have guided the Conservation Corporation over the past four years as it has evolved into Africa's premier eco-tourism company.

"Traditionally, conservation has been approached scientifically. We have developed a successful business attitude towards it to the benefit of the environment and our investors," says chairman Dave Varty, who founded the group with deputy chairman Alan Bernstein in 1990.

"We are asking companies to invest in conservation not to donate to it," Mr Varty adds.

The Conservation Corporation runs four exclusive game lodges in South Africa, including Londolozi and Phinda, three camps in the Masai Mara and Ngorongoro Crater reserves in East Africa and two Nairobi hotels.

The group is riding the wave of South Africa's tourism boom.

"We are experiencing unprecedented levels of demand," says Mr Bernstein, adding that weekly booking income has risen five times over the past year.

The majority of the guests are overseas visitors as the rates are

out of reach for all but wealthy South Africans.

Mr Bernstein says 1995 will be the first year that the group is cash positive, as a result of the surge in tourism. To date, the group has used R180-million in equity and R30-million in long-term borrowings to finance its growth.

This week the group announced a R70-million expansion programme, most of it devoted to upgrading existing operations.

Shareholders, including institutions as diverse as Britain's Hambros Bank, the Getty family trusts and AECI's Pension Fund, will be asked to provide R32-million through a rights issue.

In addition, R40-million of loan finance from the Industrial Development Corporation will be used to fund the development of SA operations.

A new private game reserve near Victoria Falls will also be added to the stable, with the help of a R10-million loan from the World Bank's International Finance Corporation.

Over the next 12 months Mr Bernstein hopes to list Conservation Corporation simultaneously in London and Johannesburg, providing further capital for future expansion.

He expects the group to be capitalised at around $70-million.

Rescuing Phinda from the Masterbond financial collapse

meeting ended and a bunch of important looking men walked out of the boardroom. Of course they saw us. The curator we wanted to see was leading the throng. He knew the office was closed. So, as I expected, he came up to us and asked: 'Gentlemen, can I help you?'

Of course I said, 'Yes,' but didn't get any further than saying who we were.

'David Varty – Varty of Londolozi,' he repeated my name, and launched into a 10-minute account of his recent Londolozi safari. 'My daughter and I were there last week. We had a fantastic safari. We saw lion, we saw leopard. All the big five.' Then he asked what we were doing, sitting outside his boardroom at six in the evening.

Now I got the opportunity I had been waiting for. 'We own Phinda,' I told him.

'Gee, that's a mess!' he replied.

'Yes, we know, but we think we've got an answer for you.'

'Shit, do we need answers! Come and have dinner. We'd better talk.'

So from thieves trying to get in the door, we ended up stating our case over dinner with the curator who was going to decide our fate. We offered to give him 60 cents in the rand and be done. We were prepared to write out a cheque there and then for R23.5 million. I told him he could go back to his meeting the next day with one less problem on his hands. The alternative was that they would be left with a bunch of bankrupt farms in the heart of Zululand where pre-election anarchy was brewing and for which they would get diddly-squat. It was a somewhat different story to the presentation we'd made a few weeks earlier about exactly the same place.

'Right,' he said.

'It's a done deal.' Phinda lived again – for the second time.

Next, we went to see Neale Axelson who headed up the AECI Pension Fund. Now we had some real ammunition.

We told him, 'Anton Rupert, chairman of the South African Nature Foundation, thinks we're bankable. We have a 20-year lease on Ngala Game Reserve, a R80 million asset in a prime location within the Kruger Park. We are developing Phinda and we've done a deal with the curators of Masterbond. We've got Phinda at 60 cents to the rand and saved the new investors R18 million. Come on! What more do you want?'

We took Neale Axelson on a boat cruise on the river at Phinda. It was a stunningly beautiful afternoon. Kingfishers, herons and fish eagles were everywhere. As the sun set and a full moon rose over the river Neale turned to me and said, 'Dave this has got to be the future.'

Next, Judge Bill Newsom arrived in South Africa. He brought Gordon Getty with him. Completing the party was Mark Getty, Christopher Sporborg from Hambros and Neale Axelson from AECI. It was a massive coup for us. We flew to Phinda, which was still a building site, and decided we would do a Land Rover ride over the property on the first day and show them the beach on the second day. We would also fly over the region in a helicopter. They had a mob of people with them, including other family members and trustees. It was a logistical nightmare. And it cost a fortune. But, we were keen to make a near perfect impression and we were lucky. That first day the weather was beautiful.

We set off in two Land Rovers. We had no radios. But all seemed well. Then Mark turned to me and said, 'There is one thing you should know. My uncle has arachnophobia.'

I replied, 'What are you talking about?'

'If Gordon sees a spider he'll leave.'

I could not believe my ears or our misfortune. 'Mark, why the hell didn't you tell me this before we set off? It's Easter. There're spiders wherever you look. It's about the only living thing you will see. We'll see thousands! In fact, right now, the golden orb spider is the highlight of any game drive at Phinda.'

So we tried to catch up with the other Land Rover and as we came around a corner, sure enough, there was Les Carlisle giving a lecture on the golden orb spider which had strung its web across the road. He had thrown a grasshopper into the web to illustrate the spider hunt. At that moment, a spider-hunting wasp flew in and stung the spider to death in front of Gordon Getty's eyes. Gordon was overjoyed and suggested that we opened reserves all over the world exclusively for the protection of the pompilidae wasps. Gordon was a larger than life character and full of fun. Later that day we took a helicopter trip, flying south to Lake Sibaya and north over the beach to the Kosi Lakes. It could not have been more beautiful, nor could the day have gone better.

The next morning, in our infinite wisdom, we planned to take one half of the party up the coast in a 'rubber duck', to a landing point known as Black Rock. The other half of the party would drive up the beach in a Land Rover. We would swap the groups on the way back. But it was very hot, 'Zululand hot', and the wind was building up. We got out of

Sodwana Bay and had an hour's boat ride up the coast ahead of us. But there was a heavy swell running. The Getty trustees, in their Gucci shoes and New York shirts, were looking decidedly uncomfortable.

As we buffeted up the coast in our rubber dinghy, many could not take the sun, the heat and being tossed around. Pretty soon one man was leaning out, retching over the side. Later he was heard to comment, 'What the hell are we doing this for?' His face was bright red and if he had anything to do with the investment, it would never happen.

Kevin Leo-Smith took quick action and made an unplanned run at the shoreline, beaching the dinghy. A shaken, somewhat lighter shade of green group of potential investors staggered out onto the beach and began to recuperate in the shade of the coastal forest. Another near-disaster had been averted. Somehow, despite the lack of radios, the other half of the party found us. We abandoned all thought of further marine activity and the day ended with a memorable candlelit dinner in the bush.

We also took the party to Londolozi and our old friend Enos Mabuza joined us. We listened while Enos articulated the future of South Africa and the model which Londolozi had developed. He believed Londolozi, Phinda and Ngala would thrive in the future South Africa – Mandela had already said so. Amazingly we had Gordon Getty, the 64th richest man in the world and Bill Newsom, the appellate court judge for California, sitting on overturned beer crates in the Londolozi staff village listening to the future possibilities in South Africa. I remember the moment when Bill leaned across to Gordon and said, 'Gordon, we've got to support this.' This was the turning point in our quest for funds.

We went barrelling back, full of joy. We had Phinda back on track, we had secured Ngala, and we remained world experts on all matters. The story did not quite end there. Neale Axelson of the AECI Pension Fund told us that if they came on board, they would want to see our Masterbond debentures repaid in full. They were not prepared to be seen taking unfair advantage of widows and orphans. After all, they were a pension fund and in the business of looking after money belonging to widows and orphans.

Then wires got crossed. Having told Mark Getty how clever we'd been with the Phinda curators, we had to explain the AECI view: that is, that we should pay back in full the amount owing – including the

Photograph: Molly Buchanan

Connecting the Mkuze wetland to the Mzinene River which forms the southern boundary of Phinda – wetland to wetland

R18 million we thought we had saved as a result of our negotiations with the curator. Mark had already told his trustees that they were getting into this investment below market value and he went ballistic. He really thought we were trying to steal from our prospective shareholders. I had seen the big sign up on the wall in Hambros' corporate finance office: it read 'Never Trust the Management' – a slogan which, until then, I had never quite understood. Mark was convinced that Dave and Alan were making a quick turn on the project at his expense. He told us that the Getty family was out! We arranged for Axelson to talk directly to Mark and eventually, after all the smoke had cleared, we sat down and signed the documents. But all we had was R39 million cash financed primarily by the Gettys and the AECI pension fund and a number of smaller shareholders. And we owed the Masterbond liquidators the lot. Incidentally, we were the only company to repay our Masterbond debt in full.

Our business was under way but we had a funding conundrum: we had a half-finished game reserve with a half-built lodge and a defunct Ngala Lodge and in effect no money for development. The project was undercapitalised and would remain that way for another decade. We had a lot of work to do on all fronts.

Johan Hoekstra 2011

AFRICA'S JURASSIC PARK

First on Phinda's agenda in 1990 was the opening of Mountain Lodge. Alan and I were, as usual, trying to raise more money to keep ahead of the cash shortage that threatened to overwhelm us and we were not there for the opening.

The next day Shan called me in London to tell me the story: the opening had been spectacular, but not in the way it had been planned. Not one, but three Zululand storms of biblical proportions collided directly over the lodge at sunset. Violent lightning continually lit up the sky and the rain came down in sheets. Before the night was out a mudslide brought half the mountainside into the newly completed cottages. All the winding paths and the landscaped indigenous gardens disappeared under the mud. It was total chaos and it took weeks to clean up the mess.

When we signed the deal to purchase Trevor Shaw's land, he had wished us good luck and told us, 'I've been here 10 years. Five of them have been drought and five floods. Good luck to you!' In our first month of operations at Phinda –May 1992 – we had 500 mm of rain.

A few weeks later the place was cleaned up and we were ready to open our doors for business. But no one came. No one had ever heard of Phinda. And no one wanted to go to KwaZulu-Natal where the Zulus were restless and the ANC nervous. There were no scheduled airlines, no easy way of getting there, and few people were prepared to pay the fancy rates that our computers had been spinning out to see lots of insects and a few animals. To cap it all, one of our visitors was tragically killed by one of the relocated lions. The tragedy was in a way symptomatic of the fact that too few people were trying to do too much with too little.

Even though we were up and running, our wildlife experience was distinctly questionable. We owned the north and the south of Phinda but there was a big chunk in the middle that did not belong to us. So we took people out of Mountain Lodge in a bus, drove them on a public road and, when we got to the northern sector, transferred them into a Land Rover to find what game there was – which was pitifully little. The bush was so thick, you could hardly see anything and the pineapple trucks still travelled through the centre of the reserve.

Slowly, the game experience came right. But in those early years, it was difficult for the rangers to maintain the interest of guests with little else to discuss but the sex life of a frog or the antics of dung beetles. Guests wanted the excitement of walking up to a rhinoceros and watching lions or cheetah hunt. That was still years away.

Yet I believed passionately that restoration of land was the way of the future for Africa. The restoration of its biodiversity and the creation of an economy based on wildlife would help alleviate poverty in remote rural areas of Africa. Investors were increasingly recognising that this was a slow process. But in the end such investments are wonderfully

The creation of Phinda
saved this unique forest

rewarding and in many other ways have returns far beyond the financial dimension.

One of our priorities was to persuade the owners of the farms that lay between the northern and southern sectors of Phinda to participate in our conservation project. We had difficulty in approaching these classic Zululand game ranchers with the concept of dropping fences and letting their game escape onto neighbouring property. The idea was anathema to them. But, with some persuasion, a five-year lease over the linking properties was signed and in time they agreed to a far more permanent arrangement, bringing their property into the

Munyawana Game Reserve, which we established along similar lines to the Sabi Sand Reserve. It was a great idea and a remarkable step forward for conservation in that region and a fundamental step towards the formation of the Greater St Lucia Wetland Park. At last, Phinda began to take shape. We were also trying to persuade the KwaZulu-Natal conservation authority to drop fences and join private sector land to the public reserves – a battle which continues to this day for reasons I know not.

Now older and wiser, I am happily resigned to the fact that wildlife will make its own running. It is such a successful land-use model in Africa and will inevitably replace unsuitable farming practices in low-rainfall areas. I believe that fences will fall and conservancies will grow. Private sector, public sector and community land will inevitably come together in a productive, multi-use, wildlife economy. It's unstoppable. Wildlife may become the political football in future land redistribution arguments, but if handled sensitively could have positive spin-offs for all involved.

Our priority to realign the road which carried the pineapple and timber trucks right through the centre of the reserve hit bureaucratic blockages. We were in the last dying days of apartheid and government departments were entirely moribund. In desperation, using a hired helicopter and flour bombs, we marked out a new route for a provincial road to run to the east of Phinda where thousands of people lived in villages established as a result of the apartheid homeland policy. The new road would give the people access to the outside world and at the same time liberate access to their region. We were now, amongst so many other things, amateur engineers subsidising the province, surveying a new provincial road which we could only dream would be built some time in the future. Such is the lot of the conservation development pioneer. A few years later, the road was built and proved to be the catalyst to improving the region's economy. It also facilitated better road access to Phinda.

Our major problem continued to be that we were cash-strapped. The activity of establishing the reserve, building market share and helping our neighbours was chewing cash. Our solution was to build more beds. The computer printout proved that adding another 32 beds increased projected top-line revenue. The plan to build Forest Lodge in the north of Phinda for an additional R6 million seemed to make sense – we would grow our way out of trouble. Our total cost per bed would be almost halved. At the same time we planned to rebuild Ngala Lodge to match our vision of a portfolio of exclusive top-end lodges. This would cost another R5 million and give us 112 beds – 72 at Phinda and 40 at Ngala. The computer models were smouldering. We projected earnings that would take us to fame and fortune in no time.

The shareholders, with some trepidation, supported this view and in 1993, Phinda's second lodge, the stunning Forest Lodge, was completed. It did not seem to matter that we had low occupancies at Mountain Lodge or that Mangosuthu Buthelezi, leader of the Inkatha Freedom Party, was threatening civil war in KwaZulu-Natal – such was our belief in ourselves, our project and our country.

We also went ahead with a new Ngala Lodge. I remember sitting around a table at Ngala. We had the project manager Geoff Ash, the architect, the architect's assistant and the assistant's assistant, the quantity surveyors and all the other professionals – altogether we had 25 people giving their opinions. Later on I went for a walk with Alan.

I turned to him and said: 'Al, I can't work with that crowd. It's just too much. I'll make you a deal. Let me build Ngala my way with a hammer and a chisel and some experienced Shangaan builders and you go and build Forest Lodge the professional way. This crowd of technical advisers aren't necessary. It's too heavy-handed and too expensive. The Ngala buildings are old. They look terrible. But they're well built. We'll put some imagination into them. We'll knock out some doors and windows and make it work.'

Alan told me to go ahead. So I took on our long-standing builder friend Gert Werf and his bush development team and we renovated Ngala. Alan took Kevin Leo-Smith and Geoff Ash and a team of professionals and built Forest Lodge. By now we had learnt a couple of things. We would hold an open forum which we called 'circles in the forest': all involved would express their vision of what they imagined the lodge and the guest experience would be like and how it would work. The communication between the 'on-the-ground' future operators and the developers was a great success. Everyone listened. This was a vital exercise to connect the operational vision to the development brief and in this way we were able to ensure that our architect was totally in tune with our ideas.

A stunning concept was created for Forest Lodge: glass houses built on platforms above the forest floor so as to reduce impact on the habitat. The design was radical and dynamic. A 32-bed lodge was painstakingly

crafted using a team of 150 unskilled local people with a few skilled professionals guiding the building methodology. The glass houses were like a Meccano set, assembled and then jacked up into place. The rare sand forest trees were left where they grew and we did not damage the forest floor with concrete pouring. Instead, the concrete was carried onto the building site in small containers.

A stunning concept was created in the forest - glass houses built on platforms above the forest floor.

The lodge opened in November 1993 – four months before South Africa's first democratic elections. It was a fantastic effort and stands today as a monument to imagination, still ahead of its time in design. People love the Forest Lodge and the wonderful interconnection with the forest and its inhabitants. Slowly beds started to fill. Soon after that Ngala was opened. It, too, looked magnificent and had come in under budget with the decor from second-hand furniture shops which gave an old-world safari style to the lodge. The landscape gardeners found leopard orchids which we hung from the acacias around the waterhole where elephants regularly drank. When the bright pink impala lilies and the yellow leopard orchids were flowering it could not have looked more beautiful.

Backed by one of the most dynamic marketing campaigns ever seen in safari, featuring the 'Big Six', (the usual Big Five, lion, elephant, buffalo, leopard and rhino as well as dolphins which are a familiar sight along the Maputaland coast), helped establish Maputaland as a new area to be added to the itineraries of those in search of wilderness adventures.

With the opening of Forest Lodge the mission to create Londolozi-type models in South Africa was a remarkable success. After a little more than three years we should have stopped to draw breath, consolidate, preserve the original vision of conservation development and built cash flows. But this was not to be.

At that time, I had pressure on me to align my interests more closely with those of Conservation Corporation Africa, after its creation and the incorporation of Londolozi within its stable. They saw Londolozi as side-tracking my attention and it was suggested that I sell Londolozi to CCAfrica. Not only had Londolozi been the inspiration for the creation of Phinda and Ngala, it frequently provided key staff members to the other lodges and was the flywheel around which the new reserves were marketed.

I was passionately committed to CCAfrica's conservation development dream and, despite many misgivings, I went to my Londolozi partners – my brother John and Allan Taylor – and prevailed upon them to align Londolozi's interests with those of the new company. It was a big ask of them to put Londolozi at the whim of outside management but they backed me and their support was unanimous. Both John and Allan are highly independent individuals and did not wish to be beholden to distant shareholders. Nonetheless, they said that although they were not prepared to sell the business, if it helped me they would sign a 10-year management contract giving the corporation the right to manage the Londolozi lodges over this period while the Varty and Taylor families continued with the care of the land and the wildlife. It was a remarkable gesture from two remarkable partners.

Now we had three safari venues: Londolozi, which was booming, Phinda, which was emerging and Ngala, the first private-sector operation within the Kruger National Park. All were amazing properties, all had huge potential to expand. Later on we built two satellite lodges at Phinda: Vlei Lodge close to Forest Lodge and Rock Lodge, around the corner from Mountain Lodge. Both have twelve beds and are charming. In the dry season elephants come to drink in the jacuzzis on the decks of the Vlei cottages while leopard tracks are frequently seen around the Rock Lodge cottages. We also put in a luxury tented camp at Ngala which has proved to be successful. These were properties where we could keep our conservation vision intact: converting dormant assets and lighting them up, creating regional economic opportunity where there was none and generating hard currency revenues in a soft currency environment. There was room to do more community work and to give individuals real scope for self-development. We were there. Well, almost. But our business was poorly structured financially and we were still walking on a financial tightrope.

Our problem was that it was going to take a long time before acceptable levels of occupancies were achieved at both Phinda and Ngala. I knew that we would need to get our numbers up and to do this we would need to reach the international tourism marketing channels. We were able to use Londolozi, which was well supported by the trade, as the hub for the first safari circuit in South Africa. We acquired two Caravan aircraft and planned itineraries between Londolozi, Ngala and Phinda for the international traveller – all leveraged off the Londolozi brand. Slowly our market share grew. But, because of the massive grassroots development costs of Phinda and the speed with which we had grown, we were not going fast enough to meet the expectations placed on us by our shareholders. We should have consolidated and corrected the funding structure, making the distinction between capital appreciation on long-term land assets and cash flows from short-term lodge operations, but we did not.

Photograph: Gavin Lautenbach

CHAPTER **TWELVE**
THE EAST AFRICAN SHOPPING TRIP

Intoxicated with our progress, we came up with a new proposal: to get into the greatest of all safari destinations in Kenya. We suggested that Africa was a risky place for investors but that 'all the presidents in sub-Saharan Africa could not have a bad day on the same day' and argued that, given the uncertainty of the pre-election period in South Africa, we should spread our risk beyond our borders.

I had my reservations about expansion: what we had achieved in less than four years from 1991 was nothing short of a miracle and all my instincts screamed, 'consolidate, consolidate, consolidate'. We were operationally stretched to the limit. But we were swept up in the excitement of the moment and the allure of spectacular East Africa was too great a temptation to resist. We also needed more money and to get it we needed to tell our investors a new story.

Alan and I wasted no time getting on a plane to Florida to meet Geoffrey Kent, the doyen of Kenya's safari industry. Geoffrey was enthusiastic about our vision and our new strategy of capturing 'the high spots of the African continent' and a deal emerged. He offered us an all-or-nothing package including some really good destinations and some questionable city hotels. The Windsor Golf & Country Club, a great hotel and golf complex outside Nairobi, and the Mayfair Court Hotel, a mediocre hotel in central Nairobi were not, in any way, core to our business. We acquired the leases on these hotels and in so doing strayed from our original vision.

In Kenya, we also acquired two safari destinations from Abercrombie & Kent: the Kichwa Tembo camp was the Londolozi of the Maasai Mara and possibly the closest in style to our South African operations. It was a great asset and a hugely popular destination. It had grown from a 16-bed camp to 110-beds and would prove to be a great investment. In my view, Siana Springs, in the southern Mara, was also a good acquisition but cattle encroachment around the lodge was growing. Both were closer to our vision, though: the Maasai were partners and we were stimulating the regional economy by making wildlife pay.

The Kenyan safari industry matured in an environment that had not been ravaged by political ideology. When Jomo Kenyatta took over in

Kenya in the 1960s, tourism, which was established half a century earlier after the visit by Theodore Roosevelt in 1909, continued to flourish. It did not have the problems that grew out of apartheid in South Africa, the civil war that erupted in Mozambique, or the doctrines followed by Julius Nyerere which closed the doors to tourism in Tanzania for three decades.

When we went into East Africa it was hugely exciting. I had watched every film ever made on the Serengeti and the Maasai Mara. Now I had the opportunity to be at the Mecca of the safari business. It was also much more than that: at Phinda we spent two years wrestling with land ravaged by pineapple farming, cattle ranching and DDT spraying. Even at Londolozi we had worked hard to repair land damaged by years of cattle ranching. Here was the opportunity to be exposed to one of the most wonderful open natural systems in the world, a land that had always been under wildlife.

Perhaps most exciting of all was that on the back of the East African shopping trip we acquired a wonderful concession in Zimbabwe on the banks of the Zambezi River and in Tanzania, a 33-year lease over the Ngorongoro Crater Lodge, perhaps the definitive beauty spot of Africa. The very old, rickety lodge on the site was still operational but needed to be reduced to rubble and rebuilt before it would fit in with our upmarket lodge operations.

I recall our first visit to this Tanzanian wonderland. There were the normal formalities of two management teams sizing each other up: 'Who are these young upstarts from South Africa coming to teach the doyens of East Africa about the safari business? We'll show them!'

David Stockdale and Peter Ngori, two deeply experienced safari managers, arranged to give us a five-course meal on the Ngorongoro Crater floor including choice wines, roast beef and Yorkshire pudding and an excellent port. All around us were outstanding examples of East African theatre. To my left I could see herds of buffalo, to my right, black rhino and in the distance herds of elephants. But, as lunch was served, a huge East African storm started to roll across the crater floor. Tanzanians are extremely hospitable and caring people and they immediately suggested that we decamp and get back to camp before we were drenched. It was now our turn to show our resolve and spirit of adventure. I announced that under no circumstances were we leaving, given that they had gone to so much trouble. Needless to say, the full force of the storm hit us while we ate the roast beef and Yorkshire pudding. Stockdale and Ngori thought it was the funniest thing they had ever seen and it resulted in a huge bonding of the management teams. As we drove out of the crater on our way up to the lodge, it grew freezing cold as it does at over 2 500 metres even close to the Equator. We were continually given alcoholic beverages, by the East Africans, to fend off the cold. The result was that for the first and only time in our entire lives, Shan and I were too drunk to attend afternoon tea and cake with visiting guests. Not the behaviour expected of the newly appointed executive management.

The A&K package also included a partnership with a remarkable entrepreneur, Lovemore Chihota, who was leading the transformation of the safari industry in Zimbabwe. Soon after doing the deal with Geoffrey Kent, we flew to Harare to meet Lovemore Chihota who, in partnership with Rainbow Hotels, a state-owned hotel group, had won an amazing concession on the Zambezi River when it was put out to tender by the Zimbabwean government. The 39 000 hectare Matetsi concession included 15 kilometres of Zambezi River frontage and was right in the heart of the so-called golden triangle, which included the Chobe River to the west and Victoria Falls 40 kilometres to the east. It was a place of wild beauty and a great opportunity for safari development. We decided that we should make Matetsi a priority and build a lodge there quickly so that we could start earning money out of the concession. At a later date we would fix the Ngorongoro lodge, which was still operational and profitable.

At our first meeting with Lovemore Chihota and the Rainbow Tourism Group we talked about how we would structure the project. I remember the head of the Rainbow group telling me, 'Mr Varty, if you think you whites are going to come in here with a management contract and drain cash flows out of our country, you're very much mistaken.' I looked at him, closed my books, and prepared to leave the meeting.

Lovemore Chihota turned to me and asked what I was doing. I replied, 'There's obviously a misunderstanding at this table. The gentleman over there believes that we have come to Zimbabwe for no other reason than to take money out of Africa. He clearly has not come face to face with South Africans who believe they are of Africa. Perhaps he does not understand our Londolozi model of care of the wildlife, of the land and of the people. Our mission is conservation development.

Photographs: Peter Siebert

Ngorongoro Crater Lodge was transformed into one of the top 10 destinations in the world

We want to advance green frontiers and make sure that wildlife pays and stays and that the local people benefit.'

It was an unbelievable meeting. The men we were talking to, including Lovemore, had all been part of the Zimbabwean political struggle. They were highly articulate and politically astute. They were of the view that we would adopt an extractive, colonial mentality which was, essentially, 'put in as little as you can and take out as much as you can'. They were not prepared for a bunch of guys who were planning to invest in their country bringing in fixed assets of 60 beds at the top end of the market. The mood changed and the future meetings became very animated with lots of political banter and repartee.

Thinking back, I recognise that we misread the Zimbabwean market pretty badly. We took the South African model to Zimbabwe. There was so much going for it. I said to Alan, 'This is like having Londolozi next to Vic Falls. What we must not do is build cheap accommodation. Let's do this right from the starting post.'

That was mistake number one. Mistake number two was that instead of building 12 beds and getting up and running before we built any more, we went right in with 60 beds – computer modelling had taken over from common sense. We should have followed the Londolozi experience of slow growth in step with demand and experienced personnel. Mistake number three was that we used dollar-based debt to finance the building. And then we were too elaborate in our design. We overspent partly as a result of having to work through the government and putting everything out to tender. On top of all that, the Zimbabwe dollar went for a loop and the 'Bob' factor, which we never could have anticipated, destroyed the Zimbabwean economy.

My prediction is that the Zimbabwe circuit – which was once so popular, especially with South Africans – will rise again, post-Robert Mugabe. There is so much going for the safari business in that country. The river will still be there and although it may take time to put back wildlife, nature will lend us a helping hand. Perhaps we may have to wait a little longer than we would like. But some time in the future, the Matetsi concession and its beautiful camps will realise their full potential. Nature is patient and its plan is clear. Politics is transient and its plan confused.

While the camps at Matetsi were under construction, Alan and I decided it was time to take a look at how to unlock the potential of our Tanzanian asset on the Ngorongoro Crater rim. After years of following socialist policies, in 1985 a process of political and economic reform began in Tanzania. Seven years later, in 1992, the president of Tanzania introduced a multiparty political system. After a slow start, the pace of Tanzania's tourism industry began to pick up.

There is so much beauty in Tanzania. With 22 per cent of the entire country under wildlife, it is the perfect country for tourism. We owned a lease over a pristine site on the Ngorongoro Crater rim with incomparable views over the crater floor 2 000 feet below us. On the crater rim large herds of buffalo regularly pass by while the birdlife is breathtaking, with a multitude of colourful sunbirds, trogons, starlings and bush shrikes.

We heard that there were other properties in northern Tanzania up for grabs and did not waste time. We set off in search of new locations which would complete a Tanzanian tourism circuit. Our first stop was a concession at the source of the Grumeti River. For me it was thrilling to see the resilience of an undamaged grassland and a natural spring so powerful that it spawns the Grumeti River. We stood mesmerised as we watched the crystal clear water pour out of the ground. This was what we once had in South Africa, before too many sheep overgrazed the Karoo and before 70 years of commercial forestry on the eastern escarpment in Mpumalanga stopped the winter flow of water into the bushveld. This was what we had traded for industrialisation and progress.

On the way back from this spectacle, we noticed a small camp on a hill and were told that it was Klein's Camp on a concession just outside but bordering the Serengeti. We drove up the hill and met the manager and found out that Francesco Stame, an Italian businessman from Nairobi, was the owner. We also learnt that there were other properties in his portfolio: Stame's company, the Archers Group, owned the Grumeti River Camp in the western corridor of the Serengeti, the only lodge in the Lake Manyara Reserve, and a place called Mnemba Island north of Zanzibar.

They told us that Klein's Camp included 27 000 hectares adjacent to the Serengeti. I was surrounded by the wildebeest migration and space. There were no fences, no roads, no power lines. Just endless pristine grasslands. My objectivity was gone. I was completely seduced by the wildness and the beauty and was totally in love with Tanzania. I argued that it was a conservation development project and was like the Sabi Sand: it was a private concession adjacent to protected land and had

Photographs: Lesley Carstens

African excellence at work

communities which needed help. It reminded me of our farm Sparta back in the 1960s when I was a kid.

We had learnt that if we wanted to get support and money for our ideas, we should let the venue weave its own magic. So the stunningly situated Klein's Camp became the venue for further shareholder discussions. Christopher Sporborg came in from London. Mark Getty and entourage arrived from America and our board members from South Africa flew in and joined us.

We all met in Arusha and flew into the Serengeti in an old 402 piston-engined aircraft that looked as though it had many hours entered in its logbook and many interesting stories to tell. On the way to Klein's Camp we were to land at Lobo Lodge in the heart of the Serengeti migration route. As we approached the runway, all we could see were zebra. A solid mass of stripes. From my perspective it was a fantasy land. More zebra than I had ever seen in a lifetime.

The excitement of seeing the vast herd of zebra was exhilarating, except for the fact that they covered the length and breadth of the runway on which we were about to land. The local Tanzanian pilot lined up his beaten up Cessna 402 for his first approach. We made our first pass literally on the backs of the zebra and were forced to go around. As a trained pilot I was partly exhilarated by these flying manoeuvres but also terrified by what this local pilot was attempting to do: he wanted to land amongst the migrating zebras. Back home a warthog on the runway was treated with caution. Now we had thousands of zebra blocking the runway. Undaunted, the pilot made a second and third attempt: hectic, low-level manoeuvres, pistons working hard in the high-altitude thin air with a fully loaded aircraft and the stall warning whining loudly. What fun! Finally we decided it was impossible to land and that we should head for an alternative runway. This would involve a three-hour road trip, which would create a logistical nightmare, given the schedules that we were trying to work to.

As the aircraft climbed, I spotted a 4x4 approaching the airfield. The driver was aware of our predicament and started to clear the runway. With some reservations, I suggested to the pilot that we have another try. We made it with zebras flashing by on both wing tips, onto the Lobo Lodge runway, none the worse for all the excitement.

Photographs: Lesley Carstens

Designing and building in harmony with nature

Once we were on the ground we drove up the hill to Klein's Camp where we sat on a veranda overlooking the Serengeti wildlife wonderland. We tabled a proposal to make Francesco Stame a $6.5 million offer for his entire portfolio of properties in Tanzania. It was a lot of money and the debate became heated. The board was deadlocked. In particular, Geoffrey Kent was against the deal, suggesting that we were overpaying for the assets.

Then two bateleurs zoomed past us interrupting our discussion. They returned, giving us a second magnificent aerial display. Christopher Sporborg, our chairman, said: 'If those bateleurs go past one more time, it means that they want us to make this acquisition.' He had hardly finished his sentence, and kow-kow, they streaked past us for a third time. Christopher said: 'That's it, I say we buy.' So we bought the Archers Group of lodges in Tanzania consisting of Klein's Camp, Grumeti River Camp, Lake Manyara Tented Camp and Mnemba Island in Zanzibar, for $6.5 million in cash.

We congratulated ourselves. We had been on a most expensive shopping trip but we had acquired the best wildlife circuit on the African continent. We had succeeded beyond our wildest dreams – or so we thought.

Dave Varty and Valli Moosa visit the Ngorongoro Crater

WHAT A WONDERFUL WORLD!

The ink was not yet dry on the paper when I got word that Klein's Camp and the surrounding land was owned not by us, but by the Ololosokwan Maasai community. Some other mildly disturbing news was that the Lake Manyara lease and the Grumeti Camp lease were illegal, and even the Mnemba Island lease looked questionable. I was about to have my first lesson in dealing with a government that had taken over from a failed socialist bureaucracy.

The Tanzanian authorities had to be notified of the change in control of the company which owned all the leases to the properties we had just bought. Only then did we learn that the Tanzanian National Parks Authority (Tanapa) rules state that if a company which holds a Tanapa lease is sold, the lease goes back to the state and is again put out to tender. So the seller had our money and we had nothing. We had to tender again – and maybe luck would be on our side – if we were to secure the camps we had just bought for $6.5 million. It seemed a little unfair.

Klein's Camp was a different story. The title deed over the 27 000 hectares of land adjacent to the Serengeti National Park, which we were so excited to have acquired, had been revoked and we later discovered that the government had sold this piece of land twice. In retrospect, I think we were naive to expect that the prestigious legal firm, Clifford Chance of London, could produce an accurate due-diligence report on a confusing title deed over land owned either by the Tanzanian government or by the Ololosokwan Maasai in Africa. We firmly believed we had acquired title to this property from the Italian entrepreneur living in Nairobi. But the legal firm was in a first world country. We were in the remote grasslands of Africa where Maasai spears ruled the day.

When we came to re-register the leases over Grumeti River Camp, Manyara Tented Camp and Mnemba Island, we were told that we could not do so. Our rights had been revoked. How did we get out of this mess? I had to explain to the Tanapa officials that

Finally the headman told me somewhat forcefully that 'This is Maasai land ...'

we were the new legal owners and that our leases should continue to be valid. We were faced with the task of unravelling a legal mess and were in danger of losing everything. To top it all, the neighbouring Maasai community at Klein's Camp was becoming increasingly hostile.

Somehow, I had to find a way to meet the Tanzanian prime minister whose responsibility it was to handle internal affairs. How I achieved this goes back to 1994, when Londolozi was asked to host the Renaissance Group, a group of elite black politicians and South African black businessmen who believed that the new ANC government should achieve full economic integration. It set the scene for a number of wonderful relationships with influential people in the new South Africa, including Thabo Mbeki and Patrice Motsepe.

Patrice became a good friend and coincidentally was sitting in my office the day the call came through that the prime minister of Tanzania had revoked our rights over the Klein's Camp lease. Patrice overheard this conversation and without any consultation leapt into action.

He picked up his cellphone and made a call: 'Hello, my darling. Tell me where is Aziz?'

Before I knew what was happening Patrice had dug our deputy foreign minister, Aziz Pahad, out of a conference in Johannesburg and told him, 'This is my friend Dave. He's got a problem in Tanzania. You've got to make a plan.'

I realised that Patrice was something else. One call from him had put together a meeting that got us back on track to preserve our rights. I also realised that South Africa was truly reconnected to the African continent and that it was, indeed, possible for cooperation and that we could work productively across our borders. Maybe a United States of Africa was part of our future.

That was it. We chartered a jet and Alan and I landed in Dar es Salaam the next morning. Parked on the tarmac were three Mercedes Benzes waiting for us, with South African flags flying. We went straight to an interview with the Tanzanian prime minister and explained our problem. He told us his side of the story and said he would put his decision on hold. In the meantime we were to meet with the Masaai to try and resolve the ownership question over the land at Klein's Camp.

The prime minister of Tanzania told me that there had been an administrative error when the title deed over Klein's Camp had been issued. As a result he advised the president to revoke our rights. We were given one option; we would have to negotiate a new agreement with the Maasai.

Every month for the next nine months I travelled for two days to reach a designated tree in the middle of the Maasai lands adjacent to the vast Serengeti. Here I waited for the Maasai council of elders. The wind blew. And there wasn't a living soul in sight. Two hours later we'd see the first bright red of a moran's shuka on the horizon. Then another. And another. Three hours after the scheduled time of the meeting there would be 80 to 120 morani sitting under the trees and then the headmen would arrive. After another hour negotiations would begin.

At times things got heated, so much so that I thought I would never see the light of another day. The way it worked was that everyone got a chance to have his say. A seven-foot moran, armed to the bloody teeth with spears and sticks, would jump up and rattle off his opinion pointing menacingly in my direction. Then the next. And the next. And so it would go on all day. I felt like Piet Retief at Dingane's kraal. Some of the Masaai, uninterested in the procedures, would pull their shukas over their heads and go to sleep. Others would wander off. It was a truly organic African affair with lots of time and room for debate and consideration of each other's points of view. Then, through my interpreter, I discovered that we were being embroiled in local politics. My case was being used for one faction to score points over another. I was told that I was not in danger, although it did not feel that way.

At the end of the day my interpreter would summarise what had been said and what they had decided. Then I would give my point of view. I told them that we would stay only if we were made welcome and if the benefits of tourism could be shared by all of us. If they didn't want us, we would leave and take our lodge, our money and our jobs elsewhere. 'We operate only in areas where we are welcome and where all can share in the benefits of tourism.' That was my story.

Finally the headman told me somewhat forcefully that I must realise that, 'This is Maasai land owned by the Maasai. Dar es Salaam does not speak for what happens here.' Given that he was surrounded by 120 morani, all armed with rungus (clubs) and spears longer than my body, I immediately agreed with him.

Eventually, after nine months of negotiation, I secured a 33-year lease with them and the project remained on track. The Maasai retained ownership of the land while we had exclusive use-rights. It was workable, enforceable and supported by all those who had been part of the process.

It was a wonderful example of the capacity of Africa's people to adapt, to consult and consider all points of view, and to produce enduring decisions. In the middle of the grassland we started up a generator and switched on the computer and printed an agreement in three languages, English, Maasai and Swahili, and we all signed.

Mnemba Island also turned out to be an absolute jewel. Alan was a great connoisseur of quality: he always wore the best hat and the best shoes. Now he was also excited. 'It'll be the greatest circuit in Africa,' he told me. He was one hundred per cent right and once again I supported him all the way. But with each and every move, our original conservation ethos was slowly being chipped away and we were becoming more and more a lodge owner and management company.

After a massive amount of negotiation at all levels and throughout many government departments, all our Tanzanian leases were secured. The task of developing what we had bought and delivering on our promise began. Keep in mind that we were still sitting on a pretty fragile business structure which needed a further capital injection to bring the new camps at Phinda, Ngala and Matetsi (which we had just completed) into line with Londolozi's status. We also had the costly marketing job of getting the new camps known to the trade and to our customers. And now we were about to undertake a huge development – the biggest we ever did – in remote and distant parts of Tanzania.

The group of lodges we built on the crater rim came to be described as the Maasai Versailles. Designed by the Italian/South African architect Sylvio Rech, and with a lot of influence and simplification from the bush boy developer, they looked like Maasai manyatta on the outside but were opulent palaces on the inside. We built two camps of 24 and one camp of 12, attempting to stay with the exclusive approach. One of Sylvio's great ideas was that he set up an ironmongery factory on site. All the chandeliers for the three lodges were made using local labour trained by artisans from Phalaborwa, a town just north of Londolozi. Everyone was learning and contributing to a world-class top-ten safari destination: the Maasai from the Serengeti, the Tanzanians from Dar es Salaam and the South Africans from Phalaborwa. It was a kind of NEPAD of our own on the rim of the Ngorongoro crater.

Thabo Mbeki flew in for a visit. We were the second largest South African investor in Tanzania behind South African Breweries. Over a glass of warm champagne in a tree house from which the views into the Ngorongoro Crater were magnificent, we spoke of the African renaissance and how South Africa had rejoined the world. We also reflected on the progress being made in South Africa. It was a great moment. But further trouble was around the corner.

We had 450 workers on site ready to move into action but with nothing to do while we waited for the gum poles to arrive. They were an essential component to the whole structure but the order had been delayed. The crater rim, at 8 000 feet, is often in the clouds and soft mist in the evening is the rule, not the exception. So we had to have gum poles that were both insect proof and wet-weather tolerant. A bridge on the road to Ngorongoro collapsed and I was told that delivery of the gum poles would take another three months. I was facing a catch-22 situation: I couldn't afford to pay workers during the delay but if I fired them I would be at variance with the complex Tanzanian labour laws and I would never again be able to put together such an unusual group of skills.

I was battling. There were no telephone lines. So I was on a satellite phone trying to get 500 treated gum poles through to us by any possible means. Eventually, after three weeks, I got the gum poles on site but they were untreated and if I had put them in the ground they were going to rot. In sheer desperation I phoned the head office in South Africa and told them to charter a 747 to fly the treated gum poles up to Arusha. The accountant advised me that I had just ordered the most expensive gum poles in the world. We even examined the possibility of chartering a military aircraft from South Africa to fly them onto the crater rim. Fortunately, before we went too far down that route, we discovered Australian technology to treat the gum poles after they had been put in the ground and I was able to get the construction teams moving.

We were also fixing Klein's Camp, Grumeti River, the lodge at Lake Manyara and Mnemba Island – all at the same time. South Africa felt as if it was on the other side of the moon. Whatever was going on down there was not my concern. I had to sort out leases, gum poles, swimming pools, taxes, labour disputes, cash, cash and cash – of which there was none.

At Grumeti I asked the construction team for a swimming pool.

'How long will it take?' I asked. They told me: 'Nine months.'

I couldn't believe it. I phoned a friend in Nelspruit who was in pool construction. He put five artisans on a plane disguised as tourists so

Photographs: Pieter Siebert

| *Lake Manyara Tented Camp underwater*

as not to run foul of Tanzanian labour laws. They arrived on site and opened their substantial Delsey suitcases which we had bought as part of the ploy. They unpacked all their building equipment, put on their overalls and I got my swimming pool in three weeks, well before the Tanzanian authorities had worked out what was happening.

Then we built a camp on the shores of Lake Manyara. Sylvio Rech, the architect, had a brilliant idea. He designed tents that were bigger and better than anything that had been done before in East Africa. We set them down at the old campsite but the tents were eight inches higher than the shadow line allowed by the Tanapa regulations. More lengthy discussions with the conservation authorities in Arusha were needed.

We discovered some excellent laws in Tanzania which protected wild areas from overdevelopment, but also some that made things very difficult. After a lot of discussion, we got around the problem. I never saw the final product because the rains came, Lake Manyara rose and the whole camp was flooded. Nobody ever slept in it. I remember telling the board not to worry: 'This is Africa. It's a flash flood. It'll be gone tomorrow.' But nine months later the campsite was still under water and was ultimately relocated to higher ground.

During the construction of the new lodges, we were on a flight to Ngorongoro Crater with the architect, the project manager, and the builder who was also the pilot. Tanzania has some interesting characteristics – volatile cloudy and misty weather, high mountains and high-altitude runways – which all novice pilots should note. Notwithstanding these pitfalls, we decided to take the flight from a makeshift runway on the shore of Lake Manyara to Ngorongoro's runway 7 200 feet up on the crater rim – a new and treacherous flight path for an inexperienced pilot We were so busy talking about the various building projects and the construction schedules that we did not immediately notice that we were getting into broken cloud. I tapped the pilot on the shoulder and said, 'Don't push it into Ngorongoro. We don't have to get there tonight. Redirect to Lake Manyara's main runway. We'll come tomorrow. There's no need to mess with mountains.'

He casually replied, 'No problem.'

A little later I noticed that we were much closer to the ground. I stopped talking building schedules and started looking at flight instruments. Then I noticed the pilot was sweating profusely. We had no rate of climb. Our air speed was critical and the ground was within touching distance. On the left all we could see were sheer mountain cliffs towering up above our plane. And because we were too heavy to climb at that altitude, our stall warning was going crazy.

On board we had an experienced South African pilot, Keith Stannard, who realised the grave danger we were in. He shouted to the pilot: 'Just keep straight and level.'

To me he said, 'It's over! We're done!'

Just at that moment I noticed below me broken ground and what appeared to be a river course. I told the pilot to turn right. Keith understood where I was going with it but realised that we could not turn without stalling. He quickly corrected my instruction and told the pilot to push the nose down before making the turn. After altering course we began a painfully slow inch-by-inch climb, flying blind in the clouds and only catching fleeting glimpses of the river course below and the menacing mountain towering on our left. After the longest 20 minutes of my life we finally broke out into visual flying conditions on top of the clouds. Our altitude was 9 500 feet. Looming up on the left-hand side of the aircraft was an extinct volcano topping 11 000 feet.

Three weeks later the same three South African heroes, architect, project manager and me, took off on a return flight from the crater rim. There had been heavy rain and the runway was waterlogged. The high altitude, wet surface conditions, pilot plus three, made the take-off in the Cessna 182 far from routine. The local knowledge procedure manual suggested that you take off downhill to get airborne, nurse the aircraft over the trees and descend into the crater which has a drop of 2 000 feet. As the aircraft gathered speed you would climb out of the crater and turn en route for your destination.

The runway was 1 000 metres long. At 950 metres the pilot realised we were not going to get airborne and aborted. We barrelled into a waterhole which had formed at the far end of the runway. The water slowed the plane down and just before we hit the trees, our Kenyan cowboy pilot performed a perfect 180 degree groundloop and we ended up facing back where we had come from, engine still running and no damage to the plane.

'What now,' I asked him as he casually taxied out of the waterhole back to the holding point of the runway.

'We'll need to try that again,' he said.

Needless to say, he left without us. I remember the lesson given to me by my flying instructor: 'The two most useless things for a pilot are the runway behind you and the sky above.'

These incidents should have been a warning to us that we should go more carefully and slow things down. But we were now on an unstoppable treadmill. We'd acquired valuable assets but they needed further investment and several years to realise their full potential. Through all of this the pressures were undoubtedly mounting and Alan and I were having a tough time together. We'd developed too fast. We didn't have enough experienced hands and we hadn't enough heads on our beds. Do we grow out of our trouble or consolidate? Those were the only choices we faced.

Market structures were different in each country. Until we got to Tanzania, most of the tours were by minibus on a hell-road from Arusha to Manyara and then on to Ngorongoro. After that you did a circuit of the Serengeti. The Tanzanian circuit had good wildlife and, when the migration was on, it was spectacular, but there were also lots of minibuses and dust. The roads had fallen into disrepair and the journey was dangerously fast and very uncomfortable. Added to that, the safari was processed and not very informative.

We said to hell with that. We had a better idea. Instinctively we knew that the way to handle these remarkable assets was to fly guests across the vast country between Ngorongoro, Manyara, Klein's Camp and Grumeti River. We planned to fly people in and out of the beautiful lodges where guests would spend a few nights and where we'd run our own game drives, South African-style. The Tanzanian tour operators blackballed us. In effect, they viewed this as a direct attack on their business. So we broke another mould and pioneered a new plan, sold it and stimulated safe and efficient travel on the Tanzanian northern circuit. At great expense and without any local support we started to organise flights.

Steadily and slowly it became apparent to tour operators in Tanzania that we were providing a better, higher-priced experience and that they could make much more by selling a fly-in circuit. A combination of CCAfrica's intervention and the Tanzanian methodology brought a better quality of experience to the area. Eventually this was to become one of the great wildlife circuits in Africa and today represents a very profitable division of the CCAfrica group.

Photograph: Richard du Toit

THE FOUNDERS' TRAP

At the start of 1996 we were stretched beyond belief. We had too many beds and not enough heads to fill them. We were too widely dispersed. We did not have enough skilled people and certainly not enough capital. And every time we raised money for a new development it had to be used to fill the holes behind us while the new project that we had taken on was starved of capital.

When we started we had a simple conservation development philosophy: acquiring dormant undervalued farms and converting them back to wildlife wilderness. This conservation ethos, supported by small, exclusive, luxurious lodge operations in South Africa, was becoming subordinate to a much grander tourism business.

Alan was not the only one stretched to his limit. I was up to my eyes trying to work with the Tanzanian bureaucracy and understand their statutory requirements. I had to wrap my mind around the Tanzanian labour and tax laws and the unknown market structures of East Africa. On top of that I was building new lodges and upgrading old ones. And I also had the job of rebranding, integrating the staff and training. Our experienced staff were spread very thin. Where to now?

You guessed it. A new deal arrived. Back in South Africa, Southern Sun no longer wanted their Sun safari lodges and a deal with them was on the table which valued CCAfrica at R300 million. Southern Sun would give us their three lodges plus R15 million in cash in exchange for 10 per cent of the company. I was told by the corporate financiers that, 'It's a brilliant deal. Just look at the value we have created in CCAfrica.' I was hugely concerned that the Southern Sun bush lodges didn't fit our profile. They were high-volume, non-exclusive operations. But we were flat out of cash, running on empty and no one would lend us any more money. We desperately need the R15 million cash injection. So we came up with a solution. We'd buy lodges costing R30 million so we could get our hands on R15 million in cash. A strange quirk of logic! It was also the second time we strayed from our vision of investing in prime locations in Africa and creating stylish small lodges for the world's most discerning travellers.

And then we strayed again. We discovered Makalali, west of the Kruger National Park. When we first met Charles Smith and his brother Jo, the Makalali lodge they owned was half-built. They were keen to get CCAfrica's involvement in the project, possibly via a management contract. I was in East Africa and was asked to come back and inspect the property. I had no illusions. It was ecologically limited, badly located, poorly designed and, anyway, we could not fill the beds we already had. In a nutshell it was something we could well do without given the rapid growth of the past few years.

I suggested that at the very most they consult with our project management team to see if anything could be done to improve the situation they were in. My view was that we should not forget that we had other priorities and I was against being involved in any way. But I was told that a management contract 'would contribute to head office expenses'. This is an old and flawed battle cry from a management team in trouble: more management contracts, more overheads, more cannabalisation of existing beds and less focus and a bigger treadmill of volume, process and commoditisation of the product. A week later we sent our project team to Makalali. The plane they were travelling in hit a mountain. The project management team including Jo Smith, the moving spirit behind Makalali, and our much-loved Geoff Ash, who had so ably guided us through the building of the Phinda lodges, were gone. Makalali immediately became rudderless.

In the wake of this enormous tragedy, we took on responsibility for Makalali. Embedded in the structures was an Industrial Development Corporation loan and a possible new route to much-needed cash. We followed the scent and raised a loan from the IDC on the back of some highly creative modelling of Makalali's future performance. CCAfrica lived on precariously and at great personal cost to all those involved.

Simultaneously with the Makalali development and using the same flawed logic that any management fees we raised would contribute to head office expenses, we took on another management responsibility. Tswalu was a massive 120 000-hectare desert reserve on the edge of the Kalahari and not far from a town called Hotashel. The name explains why it was so difficult to develop as a tourism destination. Although it was a brilliant project and a wonderful conservation effort, it was miles from any regular tourism circuit and in the short time CCAfrica held the management contract, it battled to fill the lodge. Tswalu was later bought by the Oppenheimer family and continues to operate as an independent project and to fulfil its role as a superb conservation effort especially for the desert black rhinoceros.

At this stage I was running on empty. I was developing lodges on the banks of the Zambezi River, I was building on the rim of the Ngorongoro crater, rebuilding on the shores of Lake Manyara and I was working both in the western corridor and the northern edge of the Serengeti as well as on the Zanzibar Island of Mnemba. I woke up every morning and stared at some of the most unbelievably beautiful real estate in the world – places I had only dreamed about because under our former apartheid policy, as South Africans, we had not been welcome in any of these countries. But I had lost something. I had strayed from the original vision.

I wasn't interested in making a fortune. Creating circuits was an important side of the vision but without the other side, without the conservation ethos, I had lost my purpose. I was far from home working for distant shareholders now represented by non-like-minded fund managers. And now I was flat-out lonely. I missed my family, the most important thing in my life.

We had started out with four bright, imaginative people. Trevor Coppen and Kevin Leo-Smith, the original architects of Phinda, had dropped out early. Alan Bernstein left the corporation late in 1997. In the hurly-burly years when we were fighting to give CCAfrica life, there was no way we could have survived without Alan. Phinda would have been stillborn and the remarkable Tanzanian and Kenyan circuits would most certainly not be the forces they are today within the CCAfrica group had it not been for Alan's vision and driving force. Some 3 500 people would never have had jobs, 35 000 dependants would be looking for other sources of support. When the going got tough, Alan kept one step ahead, eyes always on the horizon. He was always planning more and always on the move from one crisis to another, deal after deal, until we outgrew our financial and management capacity.

Alan Bernstein – a graduate of the Insead School of Business in Paris – is highly intelligent, articulate and has big ideas. With his business school background he was able to give Masterbond, and later Hambros, impressive financial presentations of our plans and our needs. There was no doubt that he read the market correctly. We were at the dawning of a new industry and had come up with the right idea at the right time.

South Africa was moving towards democracy and we were rejoining the rest of the world.

Alan only ever did what he believed to be good for the company. He has a true pioneering spirit and the intellect to see opportunities years before anyone else. I am certain that the Southern and East African safari industries were given a great boost under his driving influence and that the planet will be a better place for his presence.

My action in insisting that Alan leave CCAfrica was an attempt to stabilise the company and to bring reality to our projects both in the financing and the operating of the far-flung venues we had gathered together. I recall the two of us sitting with Christopher Sporborg in his office in London. He said how much he liked us both and how much we had achieved. How he wished he could bash our heads together and make us find a way forward together. To this day I regret not finding an alternative way to continue together. Sadly, Alan and I parted company. On reflection, this event marked the beginning of my own demise in the company.

In the space of eight years, CCAfrica had grown into a large organ-isation with no less than 29 lodges spread over five countries. We had acquired no less than 13 of these in as many months and many were grassroots ventures carved out of the African landscape and requiring years to become established destinations. We needed a new structure and effective controls. The value of our assets showed remarkable growth. It was a very different body to that which we originally con-ceived. Conservation had been back-ranked to the imperative of returns on investments and limiting shareholder exposure.

Steve Fitzgerald, whom I'd brought in some years earlier, was tasked with lodge operation responsibilities. With Alan gone, in 1998, I was charged with corporate funding and searching for a new shareholder of reference. I had learnt a lot from the past few years but I was in no way trained for the new task. Nor was I skilled in handling what was to follow.

Nevertheless, I reminded Tony Williamson, who took over as chair-man from Christopher Sporborg, of an earlier meeting where I demon-strated to him just how crippling the perpetual undercapitalisation of the company had been. Later on I proposed a number of alternatives to the board: to liquidate the company, enter into a trade sale, or recapitalise with an injection of R120 million but, at all costs, to avoid keeping the company on drip-feed funding.

Nine months later we were still struggling to stay alive and dri[p] feed was still the strategy. I had reached the end of my tether with t[he] frustration of trying to operate an undercapitalised business and being held accountable. The strain on one's credibility was untenable.

My mandate from the board was to refinance, refocus, and restructure. Refinancing meant that we had to reduce debt and find an investor of reference – a somewhat daunting task in the circumstances. Refocusing meant getting rid of non-core assets and giving full attention to our portolio of exclusive lodges set in beautiful wilderness areas. Restructuring meant significantly reducing head office and marketing overheads by closing the overseas marketing offices. We immediately closed the offices in Belfast, Miami and London that had sprung up in an ill-conceived direct-to-trade telemarketing strategy that destroyed our established relationships across the entire spectrum of the travel industry. We then had to start on the uphill battle of restoring the credibility of CCAfrica in the eyes of the traditional travel industry distributors.

In quick succession we got rid of Makalali, Tswalu, the Zululand Safari Lodge and the Windsor Hotel & Country Club. But I could not immediately find buyers for the Sun lodges, Tau and Bongani, and the board rejected a management proposal to cancel the Mayfair Court Hotel lease. While I had been here, there and everywhere, the head office had grown to over 200 people. Operations managers increasingly brought everything to the centre and, with few exceptions, controls were taken away from lodge managers. Central overheads escalated at the expense of resources for the operations. This directly impinged on the guest experience.

All my instincts told me that there was an opportunity to reduce central costs and improve our operations. Particularly in the light of how far-flung our operations were, I felt the need to put the entrepreneurial flavour back into field operations. I also wanted to create focused regionalised business units, and place the authority and responsibility of the guest experience and the financial success of the units in the hands of the managers who were at the cutting edge of the day-to-day operations. In fact all I wanted to do was to return to the tried and tested Londolozi model which was our original blueprint.

Most importantly, I wanted to put the bush back into the South African safari lodge experience and reduce the 'hotel' approach. Lodges are not the same as hotels. They are not a convenient place to stay overnight – complete with telephone, TV, air conditioning and a comfortable bed. They should be compared to a restaurant experience where people spend their recreational time and money and the proprietor/owner is highly visible making sure that his restaurant is a place of entertainment, theatre, relationships and hospitality. Similarly, the manager and staff of a safari lodge have to ensure that their guests enjoy every waking (and sleeping) moment. It's a delicate art and cannot be controlled by a head office thousands of miles away.

Process, discipline and control were replacing excitement, originality and spontaneity. Where was the balance? Were we in the early stages of the classic corporate life cycle – advancing steadily into bureaucratic old age? Could we find a middle path to maintain the conservation ethic, economic viability, innovative thinking and spontaneity of the guest experience? There were many things wrong with CCAfrica. There were also many things that were right. So much potential had been created but the mistakes resulting from rapid growth and poor financial structuring needed to be corrected.

When I proposed decentralisation of controls, I found I did not have the support of my operations management team. So on top of a desperate need to focus on turning the company around, a further operational divide began to emerge as the centralised control hotel culture clashed with the bush lodge decentralised system I advocated.

Tony Williamson and I began our search for a new shareholder of reference. We discovered Capricorn Investments, a subsidiary of the Hollard Group and a private equity investment arm of the prestigious and wealthy Enthoven family which has interests both in South Africa and internationally. The Capricorn Group began investing in safari with the acquisition of a tour-operating company, AfroVentures. Their vision was to combine this investment with CCAfrica's ground operations. It was at odds with my belief that we needed to downsize the business and focus on lodge operations and not tour operations. But we needed Capricorn's investment and we would only get it if we compromised further on our original vision. So, CCAfrica spent R120 million buying a tour operator and we adopted the new shareholder's vision. Once again, instead of consolidating we expanded.

I was completely overridden by the new investor's plan, which would result in expanding the business into a tour and lodge operation across sub-Saharan Africa. The mandate I was given by the board was 'to restructure the business'. I now found myself in what I called a D9 negotiation. I was buried up to my neck in sand arguing to downsize the company while the new investor was driving a D9 bulldozer 'negotiating' to expand tour operations. The CCAfrica board was desirous of managing and limiting shareholder financial exposure by bringing in another investor which would help them achieve their goal. And, in any event, the company needed money. So the inevitable happened. The millions we spent in a paper transaction greatly disadvantaged the original shareholders who, until then, had done all the heavy lifting to create the value which existed in CCAfrica. Moreover our capital shortage was worse than ever.

Now we were in tour operating with a web-based travel distribution company, a conference company and a Cape Town office. Instead of coming down, our overheads went way up. The advisers and investment analysts had a vision to form Dreamco, a company which would link CCAfrica's lodges with the tour operating business. This seemed a strange way to consolidate. But it was exactly the path that CCAfrica's management and shareholders chose to go: towards management contracts, incentive group tour operations and on-line sales. The original vision was losing ground to other imperatives.

I never wanted to be a travel company and now nobody was talking conservation development. We were tracking in exactly the opposite direction to where I wanted to go. As it turned out, after massive further capital injections by the new shareholders – double the original amount proposed by myself – the travel distribution company proved to be a good decision for what CCAfrica was to become – a major lodge-owning and management business on the one hand and an Internet travel distribution and tour operator on the other. This could never have happened if it had not been for the immense wealth of shareholders on the newly constructed board and the fact that the shareholders' advisers, who had taken the group in this direction, were now under an obligation to ensure that their plan worked.

The irony of this acquisition was that the Internet was on their doorstep and CCAfrica could have developed their own web-based marketing and tour operating structure at a much lower cost than the R120 million they paid for AfroVentures and the further R240 million they needed to inject into the business to correct their financing struc-tures. With the

| *My mother and the mother of Londolozi*

benefit of hindsight the same result could have been achieved for less capital injection. But hindsight is 20/20 vision.

I remember going to a workshop at the Leopard Creek golf estate. All the managers and directors were present and wrote up their vision of what they wanted the newly emerged CCAfrica to be. All of them wanted the company to be an exemplary tour-operating company and lodge-management company. None of the new faces had any idea of where we had come from or what had gone into the last eight years to bring us to our current position. Anyway, the past was irrelevant to their future. I was a lone voice. We had lost conservation development along the way and I had limited influence over the new direction the company was taking. Furthermore, I had virtually no equity in the company – apart from the bit I had acquired with the management contract over Londolozi – and that, with the issue of further shares in the business, was watered down. I felt that there was no place for the last of the original founders with his crazy ideas on conservation, and I was running out of any resolve to continue.

In November 2000, 12 working days before I gave the presentation to the Board proposing substantial changes to the running of the business, my mother was tragically killed in a car accident. Our much-loved 'Mother of Londolozi' was gone.

In a state of semi-shock, I began a last-ditch battle to reinstate an entrepreneurial structure and retain the conservation development element in CCAfrica. I suggested a reduction in annual central costs from over R70 million to below R30 million, an immediate injection of R120 million, a flattening of the management structure, reducing the reporting lines and the devolution of responsibility to the lodges. I was convinced there was still great potential residing within CCAfrica but only if we got rid of the massive head office which was chewing money. I still believed that an organisation carrying a big central overhead would be vulnerable to the vagaries of tourism and terrorism. My view remains unchanged today. I knew also that if I was to continue I needed to get myself back into the ownership structure. But the board was in need of managers, not a maverick founder-entrepreneur who was making various suggestions regarding an equity participation alongside the new owners of CCAfrica.

My proposals were rejected by the board and on 26 January 2001 I cleared my desk and left the building. With the exception of Tara Getty, Jon Klein and Tony Williamson, who had become good friends, not one

Cartoon: Mike Scott

My CC Africa years
The D9 bulldozer 'negotiation' with the new investors

of the shareholder representatives was human enough to stop for a moment, look me in the eye and say goodbye. After 10 years of giving everything I had to create a conservation development dream it was a sad indictment that the company appeared to have become a place of indifference to the individual from those at the helm.

A few days later I made a farewell speech to the staff members. There were tears from those team members who had been with me during the pioneering years of great adversity when so much camaraderie had developed.

But there was little fellowship from the executive managers who had cast their lot with the new generation of board members whose values were so different from my own. I felt like a castaway who had been chewed up and spat out – regardless of what had been created. At the time I felt that all I had stood for – or tried to strive for – was gone. It was clear that my work was done. CCAfrica was moving into the next stage of its life cycle. It was time for the last of the four original founders to move on.

A few months later, in April 2001, I flew to America to honour an Africa Foundation commitment. Within a few hours of my arrival in Washington the news reached me that the previous day, hours after I left, my family had been the victims of a horrendous attack in our Johannesburg home. I returned home immediately. We could only be thankful that everyone was alive, although the guards and our maid were badly beaten up and the trauma of facing a gang of thugs wielding guns for over five hours was enormous. Boyd, who was only 17 at the time, had a gun shoved into his mouth. Shan possibly suffered most. In my absence she felt the responsibility for Bronwyn and Boyd as well as Kate Groch, their teacher, who was with them that terrifying Sunday night when they faced the very real threat of being raped and possibly murdered.

I was reminded of William Shakespeare's imitable statement: 'When sorrows come, they come not single spies, But in battalions!'

REFLECTIONS ON THE JOURNEY

After the tumultuous years within CCAfrica, when I was alone with my dog, I had lots of time to recall the good times and all I had learnt along the way. There were many successes. To begin with, Phinda acted as a catalyst to the development of safari in Maputaland and for the creation of the Greater St Lucia Wetland Park which had been acknowledged a World Heritage Site in the 1990s. Since the early days when we first visited Maputaland, many safari lodges have sprung up and, in a decade, Phinda's land and land surrounding the private reserve has trebled in value.

From being one of the poorest regions in South Africa with an average per capita income of R450 per annum, the change in a decade had been sensational. Once the new road was built to the east of Phinda, the rural villages gained access to markets and tourists drove past the new craft and trade centre. A clinic was built where no health care had previously existed. Thousands of children found the opportunity to have their classes in schoolrooms rather than, weather permitting, under trees. They also had access to scholarships to attend university. And the emerging Maputaland safari industry provided jobs for many people.

Soon after the formation of Phinda, Chief Simon Gumedi, the Makasa community leader, indicated that he would plan to include some of the former homeland which lies on Phinda's eastern boundary. Later on he suggested that the Makasa community should own Phinda and in 2007 this became a reality. A deal was constructed under which the Makasa community acquired ownership of Phinda and leased it back to CCAfrica for 72 years. CCAfrica was paid at market values for the sale of the Phinda property. This transaction represents a pathfinder to future outward creative conservation in which the redistribution of land can result in a more equitable arrangement of land ownership.

It is seldom in trying to resolve the problem of land claims that a solution can be found in which all parties win. Conservation wins. Biodiversity wins. Politicians win, investors win and the community, as landlords, receive annuity cash flows every month. It's a win/win. It is to be hoped that, in the future, this road map will be followed by others across South Africa.

In my view, the world needs land-restoration investments more and more. One hundred years from now a pristine Phinda full of wildlife will still be there to fascinate visitors to Africa and will be more valuable than a landscape scattered with shacks and shambas drawing exponentially on the finite resources of land unsuitable for farming. My hope is that in the future our Londolozi model will inspire more Phinda-style investments across the world which will ensure protection of the world's biodiversity. Edward O Wilson (a microbiologist turned conservationist and adviser to US presidents) commented in his book *Living Planet* that a $35 billion investment in the purchase of specific habitat types, would protect 80 per cent of the world's biodiversity. It might seem a large number, but it is not when you consider the cost of war or the iniquitous agricultural subsidies that protect the rich nations' markets. (All up costs of the Iraqi war have exceeded $2 trillion – so far.)

Over the next hundred years I believe that many more people with wealth will take from the Getty/Enthoven example and be prepared to put money aside for lower financial returns but high planetary rewards in Phinda-type investments.

While the past decade may appear to have been chaotic within CCAfrica, the fact that we secured the high spots of Africa before anyone realised that tourism was going to be the big African industry of the future, was a major coup. Nobody else had connected the drama of the East African itinerary with the sophistication of South Africa as successfully as we did. Until 1994, South Africa was a world apart from the rest of the continent. To this day CCAfrica's northern circuit of Tanzania is unquestionably dominant, while a combination of Phinda, Ngala and Londolozi remains a top-of-the-range itinerary in South Africa. As well as these two great safari circuits, we also secured a phenomenal concession in Zimbabwe, breaking new ground by bringing the first serious black player into the tourism industry.

There is no doubt that CCAfrica, 17 years after the corporation was founded, has achieved remarkable results, and is making a great contribution to adventure travel in Africa and elsewhere. Their portfolio of beautiful properties, acquired at much lower prices than their market price would be today, will endure long after the political mayhem has passed and the original costs and losses have been absorbed. Indeed, CCAfrica may turn full circle if its financially powerful owners again insist that it return to its original ethos of conservation development. This would enable it to take its place in the battle which has now become known as 'an inconvenient truth'. Planet earth needs more investors like them.

The founding of CCAfrica and Phinda heralded a big message: the age of restoration in Africa was born. Phinda was launched in the faith that political leaders of South Africa would find a way through to democracy and that South Africa would once again be accepted on the world stage. Since then the industry has exploded and CCAfrica has set benchmarks for service excellence and has created thousands of job opportunities and hope for individuals in many rural parts of sub-Saharan Africa.

Since 1992, when Londolozi won the British Airways Tourism for Tomorrow Award, which is granted each year to the destination seen to have made the most positive impact on the environment and on rural people, many of CCAfrica's lodges have won international awards. A few of the awards and acknowledgements that were showered on them in 2007 include:

- The World's Best Hotels: The definitive guide to the greatest hotels worldwide named Kichwa Tembo number one in Kenya for its 'tranquil location in one of Africa's most cinematic landscapes', Ngorongoro Crater Lodge for its 'architecture and design that nearly rival the extraordinary natural surroundings', and Phinda Private Game Reserve for its 'unrivalled natural surroundings and seven distinct habitats'.
- US Condé Nast Traveler's 2007 Gold List included Ngala, Phinda Forest Lodge and Ngorongoro Crater Lodge.
- UK Tatler's Travel Guide listed Mnemba Island Lodge as one of the world's '101 Best Hotels'.
- Condé Nast Traveller Gold List named Phinda Private Game Reserve the best in Africa in the category of Best Hotels in the World for rooms, and Kwandwe Private Game Reserve the best in Africa for leisure facilities.
- The Tatler Magazine named Phinda Rock Lodge as one of Tatler's '101 Best Hotels'.

These awards by no means tell the full story.

The Rural Investment Fund, which spawned the Africa Foundation, started when CCAfrica created Phinda. It was part and parcel of Londolozi's model to help its neighbours and many schemes were initiated with-in the communities on Phinda's borders. Family planning and a maternity clinic, nutrition, housing, education, AIDS prevention and the encouragement of small business were all part of its activities. Chief Simon Gumedi was initially sceptical when we first told him of our plans. He'd heard it all before: white people coming in, promising the earth and then disappearing forever. We astonished him by delivering what we promised. In fact, we believed it was critical to our conservation development model. And it has been, especially with the local people helping with the prevention of poaching and their participation in employment opportunities and increasingly in management. The Rural Investment Fund was the not-for-profit arm of our business. We brought guests to see what we were doing and those guests became ambassadors and donors giving help to the rural people of Maputaland.

On top of all of this we created the Ngorongoro Crater Lodge in one of the poorest countries in Africa, and it became recognised as a top-ten destination in the world. Its leading edge, imaginative architecture differentiated it from any other location on the continent. And there's hardly a place in the world where there is a more spectacular view than from the crater rim where the elephants wandering across the crater floor look like ants to the naked eye.

We also benchmarked employment, training, service levels and community equity participation. When we took over Klein's Camp, the colonial culture still existed: give the Maasai as little as possible and take as much as possible. We did it the other way round, almost to a fault. In many cases the countries north of us were not ready for us. Often I was naive about what was going on, but I believe that more can be done and must be done to reverse corruption and make Africa stand proud on the world stage as a real competitor.

We also learnt that in East Africa we needed to have a much lighter touch on the ground. One does not need to create 180 square metres of bricks and concrete and everything that opens and shuts to keep guests happy. In these beautiful places, nature does the work and tents, which are a far cry from the camp-style shelter that you pack on your back, provide the accommodation.

Early on we learnt the importance of maintaining inspiration within an organisation. Safari lodges are far more than a numbers game. Guests set aside precious recreational time and travel halfway across the world to seek entertainment and adventure in an African theatre. The people on the ground must feel inspired to give of themselves in creating the magic that weaves a spell that will stay with our visitors for a lifetime.

The upmarket lodge experience can act as a catalyst, harnessing enormous wealth and influence from other first-world countries and bringing it to Africa. The dramatic growth of CCAfrica and its investment into Africa impressed the ANC and, as a result, we were able to influence ANC policy on conservation and water management. CCAfrica lodges also followed a model that was in step with modern requirements of management transformation, the triple bottom line which included social responsibility investment programmes.

We invented care of the land, care of the wildlife, and care of the people long before it became fashionable. On a macro level something enduring was built. It is my belief that CCAfrica can go on to be of great service to Africa and other continents, setting an example as a sustainable business in rural areas where little other economic opportunity exists. The political and economic conditions in South Africa are receptive to innovative development ideas. CCAfrica's owners should seek out its real potential beyond management contracts and tour operations.

Shan and I still find time to travel to some of the magical places that we discovered during the decade we spent with CCAfrica. Mnemba Island remains a favourite where, as part of a long-standing agreement with CCAfrica we can visit and – if we choose – do nothing but stare at the ever-changing colours of the sea and listen to guests enthusing about their safari on the Tanzanian northern circuit. It is gratifying to know that these beautiful lodges give such joy.

Life is a circle. If it deals you blows, you need to understand that the wheel keeps turning. There are times when you are at the top or at bottom of the heap and there are times when you are coming up and times when you're heading down. But you may be sure that when you get there, you will begin a journey of rediscovery. The hard times are tough. But this is when true learning takes place and when one gains a real perspective on life and one understands that much of what seems important at the time remains an illusion. What is important, no matter what life deals out to you, is to remain enthusiastic and enjoy each and every precious moment. You don't have tomorrow. Yesterday is but a memory gone. There is only the present. Make the best of each and every moment as it passes by. This has been the greatest lesson and the greatest gift of the journey so far.

The safari industry offers sustainable career opportunities for people that live in the rural parts of Africa

ISSUE NO 3   APRIL 1993

THE CONSERVATION CORPORATION
NEWS

LONDOLOZI   *Ngala*   PHINDA

Dave and Shan Varty receiving The Tourism for Tomorrow award from Dr David Bellamy.

"TOURISM FOR TOMORROW" AWARD

Londolozi has won the world's most prestigious environmental tourism award – granted to the tourism destination that has the most positive impact on the environment and local people. Competing against 64 entrants from around the globe, Londolozi was named world winner of the 1992 Tourism for Tomorrow Awards, held in London in February. The twelve finalists included projects ranging from the preservation of Trinidad's rainforests, to the protection of Austria's mountain walking areas, and Scotland's wild brown trout.

The awards – sponsored by British Airways, the British Tourist Authority and the Tour Operators' Study Group – are designed to promote environmental awareness in tourism. Last year's overall winner was designed to clean up Nepal's "toilet paper trekking trails".

The judging panel, chaired by top environmentalist and TV personality David Bellamy, announced Londolozi as the overall winner for "achieving a balance in meeting the needs of the local population, tourists and the environment".

"This type of reserve is the main chance that African wildlife has to survive," said Dr Bellamy. "Londolozi is not just about wildlife; local people also benefit and guests have the opportunity to observe a sustainable relationship between tourism and the environment."

In winning the awards, the Londolozi model – based on the principles of land restoration, care of wildlife, service to guests and involvement of local communities – is to be promoted as a model for sustainable tourism around the world.

WILDLIFE BRIEFS

Drought relief: More than 500 mm of rain has fallen in the eastern Transvaal since November. At Ngala, the Timbavati river flowed for the first time in three years, whilst at Londolozi, the flowing Sand River has saved the lives of drought-stricken hippo.

Cheetah cubs: Phinda's first cheetah cubs have been born and are thriving, despite close encounters with lion. Now five months old, t[...] in size and confidence[...]

Ngala lion cubs: N[...] cubs, born of two fem[...] four months ago, are [...] cellent viewing for gu[...] mother lions have bon[...] ensuring that all eight [...] become one big family.

Wild dogs: For the firs[...] of wild dogs has bee[...] Phinda. Thought to have c[...] Hluhluwe/Umfolozi compl[...] will hopefully make Phinda [...] extensive home range.

Bird Club: The 600 diffe[...] of birds in Maputaland (as [...] the entire continent of Au[...] attracting bird watchers [...] Phinda has recently start[...] clusive Bird Club open to [...] identify more than 200 spec[...]

FENCES DOWN AT NGALA

In a victory for conservation, fences separating Ngala from the Kruger Park have been removed – allowing a free flow of wildlife between the park and Ngala.

The National Parks Board took the decision late last year to remove all fences separating the Kruger Park from the private reserves on its western boundary. To date, most of the fences along the Timbavati reserve[...]

extend the Kruger Park by some 15% westwards and enable grazing animals to re-establish migratory patterns.

Although Ngala had fallen under Kruger Park management since being donated to the SA National Parks Trust in 1990, the 14 000 hectare reserve remained fenced off from the park until March 199[...]

WHERE DO I GO FROM HERE?

I wanted to get on with my life and continue along the road I had planned – that of continuing to be involved in the promotion of conservation in Africa. But my chief weapon, the platform from which I had launched the original CCAfrica vision, Londolozi, was locked into another five years of the management contract with the big 'nasty' corporation that had just fired me. At first it seemed like a huge and frustrating waste of time sitting on the sidelines and waiting for the contract to end.

But Shan and I soon discovered that those years, which distanced us from the immediacy of Londolozi operations and the memories of CCAfrica, were a gift. We were given the time and the opportunity to discard the stress of the past and be very clear on how we would move into the future. Most of all, we were able to rebuild strategies with which we would launch our new model and the values under which we would want a future Londolozi to operate.

We were glad that we had enlarged our ownership of land within the Sabi Sand with the purchase of Marthly which lay directly across the river from the Londolozi lodges. The land had been put up for sale by the Mala Mala group and this was a great opportunity to protect the long-term future of the Londolozi traversing area. It was a major investment for us, and in hindsight it was an inspired decision as it secured undeveloped wild lands in the heart of the Sabi Sand for Londolozi's future traversing. It was in partnership with Doc and Jenny Watson that we were able to acquire this property and we were extremely lucky in finding such outstanding partners and the beginning of a friendship which has already endured a decade. Both Jen and Doc love the bush and Doc, who studied zoology at university, has a passion for leopards and photography, which is infectious. We hope that he and his family will enjoy generations of joy from their patch of bushveld.

I recalled that my mother was overjoyed when we acquired Marthly. She remembered that our father always wanted to buy this farm but he never had the opportunity to do so. Sixty years later we carried out his plan.

Rare sighting of leopards mating.

When we asked her, what she thought of the investment we proposed, she never even enquired about the price. She just said: 'Absolutely, go ahead!' She had great wisdom and did not hesitate to agree if it meant that it ensured the safety of Londolozi and she always adopted the long-term view.

With the financial obligation of paying for the Marthly property, there was a lot of temptation to continue with the CCAfrica contract for another decade. We had a fantastic offer from them. We also knew that if we were to pick up the reins again there would be a lot of hard work for both of us. We did not know whether the travel industry would discount us as 'has-beens', or whether they would be delighted to work with us again after an absence of 13 years. Were we prepared to face the ups and downs of the international safari business? What if we faced another 9/11? Or another devastating drought caught Londolozi in its grip? We could not bank on help from Bronwyn and Boyd. They still had a number of years to go before they completed their formal education and we did not want to push them into our dream. We wanted to give them the time and space to make up their own minds about their future.

When we returned to Londolozi, we wanted, in many ways, to turn back the clock and have our old Londolozi on its feet again. But we needed to take account of the new awareness that has spread across the globe. In the wake of this, new opportunities were emerging and great conservation progress was being made. Our task was to ensure that the changes we made at Londolozi would benefit our guests and were in step with these emerging trends. What it amounted to was going much further and taking Londolozi forward to a new frontier in wilderness connections – of which we were hardly aware two decades before. But, for a while, I was needed elsewhere.

When I stepped out of CCAfrica, my brother John was already R3 million into a new conservation development project. In the early days I had handled film distribution for John. For a decade my commitment to CCAfrica had been so total that my contribution to our Londolozi Productions partnership had been limited. Now John was blazing ahead making films and I found another chance for us to work together, each making a unique contribution to the project. I started to give the production company more structure and brought in financial people to set controls and budgets. John's hare-brained ideas had so much potential but I wanted a company that worked.

John's brilliant vision was to take a piece of overgrazed land on the Gariep River in the heart of South Africa and set up a global tiger experiment. This would be the drawcard which would result in the creation of a new and exciting game reserve – eventually covering 200 000 hectares – perhaps the 'Serengeti of the South'. The aim was to restore the habitat until it became as productive as it had been earlier in the last century, before 40 million sheep started to trample the Karoo and eat the grass until there was nothing left. John planned to restock the land with the prey and predator species that once lived there.

This was another Phinda with many other exciting facets connected to it and with just as much, if not more, potential. It was possibly the most ambitious, exciting and advanced thinking on conservation that had ever come out of Africa – if not the world. And, as is normal in our society, the reaction to such advanced ideas was an avalanche of criticism, particularly from the academic world of conservation who had spent millions of dollars on global tiger conservation with very little to show for their efforts.

Scientists had spent years studying tigers and looking at the so-called subspecies. In fact, recent DNA studies have shown that the genetic variation between the different 'subspecies' of tiger is less than the differences found in cheetah populations across Africa and have proved that, with the exception of the Sumatran tiger, there is only one species, the Asian tiger. The global tiger experiment was intended to prove that securing habitat for tigers was more important than studying subspecies. As John saw it, there was only one problem: 'We had taken their space. Give them back their habitat and make sure they have prey species to eat and the tiger will thrive.'

After a very shaky start (John battled to get permission from provincial authorities to keep the tigers), he acquired a farm in the Karoo. This was ideal country for a game reserve. People like Richard Cornwallis Harris had written about the land north and south of the Gariep River a century and a half ago saying that it was the most exciting game country they had seen in Africa. In 1861 it had been the site of the 'greatest hunt in history' when a hunt was laid on for the teenage Prince Alfred, son of Queen Victoria. Twenty years later, in 1882, most of the Great Karoo had been enclosed with wire fences to camp domestic cattle, sheep and goats. The hippo, Cape lion and quagga disappeared from the Karoo – the latter two were extinct. The bushman's grass that had once fed

Photograph: Richard du Toit

Returning to Londolozi with the help of our enduring partner

million upon million of springbok had disappeared and the grasslands had been reduced to virtual desert. Everywhere one looked one found abandoned homesteads. Philippolis, just to the north of the Orange River, was on its way to becoming a ghost town. Unemployment and AIDS were rife and the population of the whole area had gone down to two people per square kilometre.

I could think of no better place to start a conservation development programme. We were brimful of ideas. There was a lot of work to do. But while I helped John, my priority was always to return to Londolozi and make it all – and more than all – it had been.

CHAPTER SEVENTEEN

THE FAMILY

I would best describe John, my brother, fondly called JV, as a mono-focal conservation pioneer. It was during varsity days that he started the Londolozi safari business. A short summary of his unique, adventure-filled life would start with lion hunting when he was twelve, organising wilderness trails for school children before he was twenty, then open Land Rover game viewing, professional hunting, animal relocation, land and habitat restoration and management, anti-poaching operations in Kenya, film-making all over Africa, South America and Asia, living with a lion, living with leopards, living with the Maasai in the Maasai Mara, with the Eskimos in Alaska, and now living with tigers in the heart of South Africa.

Throughout his adult life John had always come up with new frontier ideas. Some worked, some did not. Some were brilliant while others were crazy. But all were on the edge of reason and in most cases became new trends in conservation.

When John went to Kenya to find solutions to the disappearing game at Londolozi, he was mesmerised by the wildlife and their migrations. He brought back many lessons that were critical to our land repair strategies and which became part of the Londolozi model. At the time that Londolozi was under repair, JV met Rick Lomba and together they raised a million rand to make a film called 'The Frightened Wilderness' which was about the Botswana veterinary fence line. In exchange for his consultancy, Rick gave JV a camera and he was on his way into film-making at a furious pace.

JV always said that he was a conservation communicator rather than a classic film-maker. He understood intuitively what it is in a film that stirs emotions and excites people. Most of all, he has the ability to inspire children's imaginations and engender their interest. Many of his films were adventures which were often far removed from the more conservative style of communication of scientists and conservationists. He was heavily criticised, but this did not stop him from crossing the lines, creating heroes in conservation and inspiring young people to love and learn about the wilderness.

The Londolozi family welcomes you!

JV's filmmaking took him and his camera team into the heart of the Maasai Mara grasslands. By his side was Elmon Mhlongo with whom he developed a special relationship. Later on JV set up a cattle business with two Maasai brothers, Lakakin and Karino Sukuli, who also doubled as camera assistants and on-screen characters in his films. The unusual partnership in Kenya has lasted over two decades. JV's relationships with Elmon, the Maasai and a wide diversity of people in conservation are enduring. But his forays into mainstream society are often fraught with difficulties. Like our father, he has little patience with inconsequential social chit-chat and people without purpose. On the other hand, he enjoys a wide circle of friends who follow his conservation endeavours with great interest.

During his years of filming in the wild, JV had his share of frightening experiences. In the Maasai Mara he and Elmon were charged by a buffalo but managed to reach the safety of a tree. In their haste, they left a camera standing in the open and the buffalo turned his temper on the camera. On another occasion while John was filming on the Sand River at Londolozi, he was focused on a giraffe which had slipped in the river, and while he was filming its recovery he did not notice a crocodile sneaking up behind him. Only his sixth sense made him look up from his camera seconds before the crocodile snapped its jaws on his legs. And I remember the night, thirteen years ago when the phone rang: 'Your brother and his team are down in a helicopter in a remote part of the Luangwa Valley. We understand that they're alive but trapped in the machine.' We reach John, Elmon and the rest of the party eleven hours later. The helicopter had lost its tail rotor and went down fast and it was only brilliant flying by the pilot that prevented any fatalities.

'Silent Hunter' was the second of the 63 films that John made. When it was first shown in 1984, it was described by the buyer from *National Geographic* as 'a travesty of documentary film-making and a disgrace'. That same year, the head of Discovery Channel, as an afterthought, bought the film and when aired it got the highest rating of any wildlife documentary film previously shown on their channel. It won the Golden Grapes award in Los Angeles in 1985. Sixteen years later the founder of 'Animal Planet' told me that it was this film that gave him the inspiration to set up a television channel showing people and animals interacting on screen. John took one project at a time to the exclusion of everything. 'Silent Hunter' was followed by 'Living with Leopards' made for TOP, Turner

Original Broadcasting – yet another cat release into the wild. After that he made a 52-part TV series called 'Bush School' which was presented by Shan and was distributed worldwide by Disney. It made a significant contribution to global conservation consciousness. Those young children in South Africa who watched the show are now adults and are demanding a remake for their kids.

Then it was on to 'Shingilana', the little lion, a two-hour show about John and his partner, Gillian van Houten, living with a lion cub in the wilds of Africa which was made for M-Net, a pay television channel. Then on to bigger and better things: he decided to put more theatre into presenting wildlife to the world. The result was a feature film called 'Running Wild' starring Brooke Shields, Martin Sheen and more orphan leopards. John's ideas were never small. Now he was Hollywood in the bush. It succeeded and we still own the rights to the full-length feature film.

John continued to push the envelope on documentary film-making and leveraged the profile of tigers to world audiences – just as we had done with the leopards of Londolozi. Since the launch of the two-hour Discovery Quest film, 'Living with Tigers', John's website records more than 30 000 hits a week. His message is simple: to create space for tigers in their natural homelands where they will be safe from people and agriculture which have reduced their numbers to the point of being in danger of extinction. John also showed that it was possible to take the worn-out land of the Karoo and bring it back to life. What potential! But, out of the blue, this great conservation initiative was derailed and John and I were caught in a legal battle with one of the funders. So far we have wasted five years in courtrooms trying to preserve our good name and our rights.

It has been a devastating setback, testing one's resolve to the full. We have learned that the quest for the truth, via the legal proces, is a difficult and arduous task. It has been a harsh lesson in litigation and one which we would not wish to repeat.

In the meantime John has now formed JVCats and continues with a project called 'Tiger Canyon' near Philippolis where at full moon you can enjoy a Bob Dylan style 'Concert in the Canyon', and arrange to spend a day with the tigers which have been released into a large fenced area. It is an extraordinary experience not easily replicated anywhere in the world. For me the most significant feature of John's

| *John Varty and Elmon Mhlongo bringing Africa to your living room*

tiger project is that it will point towards a future direction for tiger conservation in Asia.

Despite the problems, JV keeps going. He is now a senior elder at Londolozi, directing our ecological activities and aiding and teaching a new generation of conservationists and guides. As a trustee of Londolozi he continues to work with Shan and me on the safari business we started 37 years ago. He has over the past decade invested enormous time in attending to his beautiful daughter Savannah and, more recently, the twins, Sean and Tao. He is truly an inspiring father in the good old-fashioned way.

The golden thread that runs through my story is Shan. When I first met her she was a knock-kneed convent schoolgirl wearing a panama hat. Since then she has been by my side giving me love and support for close on 38 years and has been a stalwart when the going has got tough. She pioneered the safari business and was the architect of Londolozi becoming a member of Relais & Châteaux. She was also a founder of CCAfrica, a founder-owner of Londolozi Publishers and a founder of the Future Nature company. Shan was a Business Woman of the Year finalist in 1994.

Shan trained as a speech and drama teacher and studied human resources. Using this knowledge she has run many leadership courses and, as a director of CCAfrica in the start-up years, she held three portfolios – marketing and sales, operations and human resources. Her contribution to CCAfrica was significant but she was intolerant of the politics and power plays which inevitably seem to develop in organisations as they grow. So, in part to stay out of the world of corporate politics, and in the belief that her departure would reduce friction at the leadership level, she elected to depart from CCAfrica in 1997.

Shan has a great love of people, but perhaps her greatest talent is her depth of understanding of the human spirit and human frailties and her ability to read people well. She has a great gift for friendship and is one of the most caring people I know. She is also an empathetic listener, a healer and a counsellor. Nonetheless her friends will tell you that, if the need arises, she can diplomatically tell you to 'foxtrot oscar' and, more than likely, you will enjoy the ride. Shan is both the glue that keeps the family together and the threads that link us to people all over the world. She is a pilot, a mother and my best friend.

| *The golden thread that runs through my story is Shan*

Shan is a great adventurer and has travelled widely, visiting the gorillas in Uganda, the polar bears in the Russian waters of the Arctic, and the tigers in northern India. She has also walked across the Maasai Mara and travelled in the Selous National Park in southern Tanzania. For Shan, these journeys are about learning. In the Arctic Circle she experienced the stark reality of the steady change in our global climate and learnt the terrible tragedy that awaits the polar bears as the ice melts and they are unable to swim the wide stretches of water between ice floes. In India she also had the opportunity to visit Ananda, rated the best health spa operation in the world where a philosophy of life is linked to health of mind and body. Many of the ideas she has collected along the way are now finding a place in the new Londolozi.

There have been many tough experiences that Shan has had to face. Apart from the woolly-necked stork coming through the windscreen of our aircraft when we were about to land at Richards Bay and the ordeal of facing armed robbers in our home, she had to cope with a forced landing of our Cessna 182 in Zimbabwe. Boyd's comment, once we were safely on the ground, was that he was impressed by his mother's emergency landing procedures, but he wondered why he was asked to put on his life jacket when the nearest ocean was a thousand miles to the east! On her second ever landing in Londolozi, Shan was unable to shut off the power on landing due to a mechanical fault on the throttle cable and she barrelled down the runway with all her 54 kilograms standing on the brakes – to no avail. She ended up hitting a marula tree. When I ventured that this was an expensive way to clear the bush, she cried for a week.

Shan also confronted a python when she went to fetch a bottle of wine in the Londolozi storeroom. She's been bitten by a scorpion, run cheek to cheek with a mamba and past elephants that have appeared out of nowhere. Bringing up children in the bush can be pretty frightening at times and can only be laughed about long afterwards. Lions in the garden, elephants in the swimming pool and leopards passing by the front door of her home required close vigilance of the kids at all times. Shan took snakes, scorpions and spiders in her stride and has always been a caring mother and a true pioneer.

The joy of our marriage has been Bronwyn and Boyd. How fortunate we were that in the early years our family formed a close-knit union. Londolozi was our home and both Shan and I had all the fun and pleasure of having our children grow up by our side. Bron was still quite

Closing the circle Dave and Shan – and the new generation – Bronwyn and Boyd

young when she started going into the Londolozi kitchen and learning the business. Boyd spent as much time as he could with me when I went into the bush to inspect the land and the animals. He developed a great empathy with the natural world and also spent many hours with his uncle who gave him a unique upbringing in the bush.

The demands of birthing CCAfrica meant that Shan and I spent more and more time away from Londolozi. I remember the devastating day when I took my kids to boarding school and the enormous emotional trauma of that experience. One night when I was in Tanzania I came to the realisation that I had made the classic western businessman's mistake. I was forty years old. My kids were eight and 10 and were at boarding school. I asked myself: 'What the hell am I chasing?' and 'What will the consequences of my life choices be to my kids who in six short years will be beyond my influence? These are the last years when I will be able to influence the values and characters of my most precious assets.' To all readers out there to whom this story may have a familiar ring, I must tell you that I made the smartest decision of my life.

The next day I called Shan and said: 'We're no longer going on as we have been. It doesn't work. We'll take the kids out of school, find a teacher for them and journey together as a family. We'll take them on a roller-coaster ride from high spot to high spot in sub-Saharan Africa.' Mnemba Island, Ngorongoro Crater, the Zambezi River, Serengeti and Phinda were some of the 'classrooms' where Bron and Boyd pursued their schooldays. Added to this, they visited the Taj Mahal in India and Uluru in Australia which gave them a rich diversity of learning about the world and its people and will live with them forever. It also strengthened our family bonds and was the greatest investment I ever made.

Once I had decided I wanted my family with me wherever I was in the world, the next step was to find a way to achieve our plan. We discussed our ideas with the headmistress of St Stithians who went along with the concept of distance learning. Although our children would travel widely in Africa, they would write their exams under the academic 'umbrella' of St Stithians. We will always be thankful to David Wilde and Ann van Zyl, headmaster and headmistress of St Stithians, a private school in Johannesburg, who completely supported this idea. We are also extremely grateful to these two educators who introduced us to Kate Groch, the teacher who travelled with us to these exotic locations and for over a decade guided the educational curriculum of our children.

The exercise of distance learning taught us a number of things. First of all, we could continue to influence our kids. Secondly, we established common ground when they walked the road with us. We found that they understood our world and there was so much we had in common that we could discuss with them. They also had a mad uncle who was making films and they could join him and do things like living with lions and leopards. We gave them the opportunity to be themselves and develop their own personalities. They did not have to conform to school requirements. We gave them space: to discover and to feel. This gave them a richer, broader view of life and they were not starved of emotion.

In Kate we discovered a gem. She travelled with us for several years on the children's distance learning programme. Including a three-month stint at the Lawrence School in Shimla in India. Then we put Bron and Boyd into Uplands High School at White River – not far from Londolozi where Bron became head girl. I remember Bron, Boyd and Kate sitting at our home in Sunninghill. They had their photo albums out. I sat on the outside and listened. They laughed and joked and looked at every page that recorded their lives together. They had fun – and they adapted well. I wondered why Boyd had gone back to school when we had found a formula that worked. So, at the end of that year, we took Boyd out of school a second time. Bron had already done her matric but we stole another year with Boyd during which he completed a rangers' course and we walked in the Serengeti and Ngorongoro Crater together.

This rock solid foundation and the bonds that developed was what caused my family to be unshakeable. So when Dad hit the rough times there was never even a glimmer or a feeling of anything but total support. Bron thinks her dad can do no wrong. Of course, she's wrong. But I have incredible family support – an irreplaceable gift which will get you through anything.

Since leaving school Bron has completed a degree in business communications which was the grounding for her new position as marketing and sales manager of Londolozi. With the family back at Londolozi, Bron has been quick to find this to be her own niche. She has left the kitchen behind and has taken like a duck to water to branding and marketing. She has also contributed greatly to restoring style and elegance in the Londolozi camps. Most of all, she has a natural and genuine warmth and interest in people that serve her as well in her communications with the travel industry and the media, as when she is hostess at the front door welcoming guests to our home in the bush.

Boyd has already had a lifetime of drama and excitement thrust on him. When he was a youngster, a mamba took a stroll over him. It was his training – he had to keep dead still – that kept him alive. When the family was exposed to a horrendous attack at home, Boyd had a loaded 9mm pistol thrust into his mouth. Although only 17, he once again kept his cool. When travelling in the Amazon jungle, he was nearly knocked out by a falling tree and was then involved in the rescue of a tourist who had fallen into a boiling hot spring. He could do nothing as the poor man died in his arms. While at Londolozi he was attacked by a crocodile in the Sand River and had the presence of mind to hold on to roots growing in the riverbank until for a split second the crocodile opened its mouth and he could pull his leg out of its jaws and, with the aid of Solly Mhlongo, leap to safety on the river bank. Boyd has grown into a young man able to cope with extreme situations, and yet remain calm at all times.

Boyd has completed a university degree in psychology and now plans to investigate the relationship between the human spirit and the energies of nature. That's where his interest is. He is investigating new frontiers in meditative walking in the wilderness and taking guests into a new space where they may find new answers to old problems. He is about engaging the consciousness and intellect, about healing of the earth and the soul. He is a philosopher giving the most spell-binding bush experience, starting off with poetry reading and silent moonlit walks past elephant herds, impala, zebra and even giant eagle owls. He is also what we call our 'impact player' called in to wow visiting travel agents and tour operators in a boma evening of great hilarity where he explains to the ladies the wide and varied virtues of the khaki-clad Londolozi game rangers.

The distance learning idea was picked up by Shan and Kate Groch and formed the basis of a project called Future Nature. Under the guidance of Kate, for a few days or a few weeks, programmes are run in parallel to formal school education. Future Nature is an attempt to inculcate into young minds a greater empathy with nature, a greater empathy with community, a greater tolerance for cultural diversity, and a greater care for the planet. It comes from the lessons we have learnt along our journey and I believe that if kids can be exposed to these philosophies the world will be a better place in the future.

I remind parents of the words of Bob Dylan's powerful song of the 60s, 'The times they are a'changin'.

'Mothers and fathers throughout the land,

Don't criticize what you can't understand.

Your sons and daughters are beyond your command.

Your old world is rapidly fading.

Please get out of the new world if you can't lend a hand.

For the times, they are a'changing.'

The unsung heroine who has been at our side for the past three decades is Shan's youngest sister, BJ Watson. I know of no one who has a better grasp of the wide range of safari lodge operations. She has worked at reception, marketing, sales, guest relations, management, training, human resources and lodge development. She is also a wonderful entertainer, full of fun and, like her sister, at times naughty and mischievous. Londolozi's Varty Camp, Founders Camp, Tree Camp, Pioneer and Granite; Ngala's Main Camp; Phinda's Forest, Mountain, Rock and Vlei lodges; Matetsi's River and Safari Camps and the five camps at Makalali are just some of the safari developments which have had the benefit of BJ's deep and practical understanding of the vital relationship which must exist between design and development of lodges and smooth operational flows.

All over southern Africa BJ is greeted with smiling African faces on her arrival. Many of these people, drawn from rural areas, have been given a vast array of service skills as a result of BJ's teaching over the years. She has cut a wide swathe in safari in southern Africa and continues to cajole, teach and train rural people in the art of service excellence at Londolozi. She too has come the full circle and recently was tasked with using Varty Camp at Londolozi as a hospitality management training facility working towards the development of senior black managers for the safari industry.

Bronwyn and Boyd Varty, the fourth generation

Photographs: Heidi-Lee Stöckenstrom

BJ Watson, project manager at work and the unshakeables – Boyd, Bronwyn and Shan

Photograph: Elsa Young

CROSSING PATHS

For both Shan and me the highlights of our journey have been the opportunity to meet many wonderful people. Just a few who have appeared on the pages of this book are Bobby Lawrence, who brought us into contact with Enos Mabuza, who in turn put us on the right road to integration of our multiracial workforce at Londolozi, and other members of the ANC, and the ecologist Ken Tinley who, in the 1970s, was years ahead of his time. So many of the friends we made contributed to the forward movement of macro-conservation issues, and many others, in some way or another, enriched our lives and contributed to the soul of Londolozi. Apart from the magic that Nelson Mandela wove for all of us when he visited Londolozi before he became president of South Africa, here are a few of the people who made a difference to our lives.

Gordon Getty – a man with real values

Gordon Getty, supported by his lifelong friend and adviser Bill Newsom, and his nephews Mark and Tara Getty, were the champions of the Getty investment in CCAfrica. To me, Gordon was a very perceptive human being and was highly entertaining and intelligent. I met him on several occasions, each of which was a great experience. He was always alternate in his views, always positive and always wished to set matters right for those around him.

My first meeting with Gordon was at Phinda when a spider-eating wasp came to our rescue and saved us from the possibility of having Gordon, who suffered from arachnophobia, cutting his ties with CCAfrica even before he got involved. I next met Gordon in Italy. Mark invited us to this wonderful place – an old family farm where he had grown up – near Sienna. While we were there the family came to visit. Gordon arrived with Bill Newsom and Bill's brother. They were all old school mates. It was probably one of the funniest evenings I have ever experienced – all were really bright men with great wit and humour. Neither Bill nor his brother was in awe of Gordon. During the evening Bill's brother said: 'Gordon, you're an arsehole!' Gordon turned to his friend and replied: 'It's for holding opinions like that about me that I regard you as one of my greatest friends!' Few people would tell Gordon exactly what they thought.

During the evening Gordon asked me where I came from. I told him I was from Africa and for the next 20 minutes he gave me a blow-by-blow account of the Phinda model and all the good things about CCAfrica. Eventually Mark, who was sitting further down the table interceded: 'Gordon, that's the guy you've invested in. He's the fellow who brought us the investment.'

Unperturbed, Gordon responded: 'Oh! Oh! So we own CCAfrica. Jolly good show.'

'No, Gordon,' Mark continued, 'we don't own CCAfrica, we're one of the investors.'

'Good thinking Mark. Bring some others alongside us. Let's all do this together.' Turning to me he said: 'It's fine work. Jolly good what you're doing down there in Africa. You're our man. We're right behind you.' With that he raised his glass of wine and announced to his assembled friends that he would recite 'Ulysses'. From memory he delivered a spellbinding oration. For a while all his friends were silent. When he finished you could have heard a pin drop.

I met Gordon again at Matetsi. We were sitting on the banks of the Zambezi updating him and his financial advisers on CCAfrica's financial performance thus far. Everyone was pretty glum because nobody liked to give Gordon bad news, especially if you're a fund manager and you have lost some of his money. I was not so nervous. I thought we'd not done all that badly because I was looking at the beautiful assets which CCAfrica had assembled in different parts of Africa. But Gordon's advisers were looking at the bottom line and that said the business lost $5 million in the last year. Gordon listens to all of this and hears the advice his people are spelling out: 'We don't think CCAfrica should have any more money.'

Then Gordon looked up as a herd of elephants crossed the Zambezi River in front of him and said: 'Look where I'm sitting. I'm in this beautiful place. I remember I made an investment in a hotel on an island off the west coast of America. That operation lost $70 million in two years. Now that's what I call a loss! This is not a loss. Keep turning the chips. Keep putting money in. My view is that this project has great potential. Now shall we go on a game drive?'

The next occasion I met Gordon was when I travelled to San Francisco to tell him that we wanted money to buy the Tanzanian properties – a big investment and one which was as yet not supported by all the shareholders. When Jon Klein and I arrived at Gordon's house, there were a lot of people milling around. No one took much notice of us. Then Gordon told everyone: 'Come on, we need to sit down and listen to what these gentlemen have to say.' While the family assembled around us, Jon and I found a footstool on which we sat rather uncomfortably, each with one cheek on and the other off. We had our presentation charts balancing precariously on our knees. We were there to tell them about CCAfrica's proposed investment in Tanzania.

As I mentioned the words 'Ngorongoro Crater' one young member of the family interrupted: 'Ngorongoro Crater, I went there in 1988; I saw a chimpanzee there.'

Another family member flew into him saying: 'There're no chimpanzees at Ngorongoro Crater. It must have been a monkey.'

'No,' came the reply. 'It wasn't a monkey, it was a chimpanzee. Or maybe it was a gorilla. But it wasn't a monkey.' A 20-minute family debate ensued.

We were only on slide two of a 25-slide presentation and the time had drifted by. It was now midday and Gordon could see that his idea of having a harmonious family gathering was not going to plan.

He quickly changed tack. 'Well, whether it's a monkey or a chimpanzee, I'm hungry. Let's go to lunch.'

So we headed off to a local restaurant where Gordon could watch the ball game over a meal. When we arrived the party got split up and I found myself isolated down one end of the table with no one interested in talking to me. Opposite me was the youngster who started the monkey argument. Just after we sat down his girlfriend arrived. She said to him: 'What did you do this morning?'

This guy, half my age, after hesitating, replied, 'Mmmm. I don't really know. We had a sort of puppet show this morning!'

After lunch I returned to the airport for the 34-hour flight back to South Africa. But Gordon supported the investment and I guess it was worth it. I have fond memories of Gordon who does so much to make the world a better place.

In 1994, soon after we got under way with the Ngala concession, I invited Dr Robbie Robinson, CEO of National Parks, to join us for a weekend at Phinda.

After dinner in the boma we started a serious discussion about fences, notably the western fence between Londolozi and the Kruger National Park. The coffee cups got cold while we continued long into the night debating the subject. Robinson and I got on like a house on fire and we enjoyed a robust debate. I was very clear. I wanted the National Park to remove the fence separating wildlife from wildlife on the Kruger Park's western boundary.

Eventually, at about two in the morning after a long day, I said to Robbie, 'Tomorrow morning when we meet, if you can bring me one ecological reason why you won't take down the western fence, I'll stop arguing with you.'

The next morning when we met for a 5.30am cup of coffee, Robbie's opening words to me were, 'You bastard! I haven't slept a wink. I can't think of a single valid ecological reason why we should not take the fence down.'

And in true character Robbie went back and removed the fence. He did it without the approval of the board and it may have been to the detriment of his career. In fact, he was the Gorbachev of national parks and he lost his job like the Russian president because he did not conform to the hard-line approach. Robbie was the catalyst to Glasnost, leading the way from the closed thinking of the past to the current enlightened ideas within South Africa National Parks (SANParks).

Just one of his many accomplishments was the founding of the Otter Trail along the southern Cape coast. He was also far-thinking and looking to where SANParks would be in 50 years' time. He wanted the parks to be the preserve of wildlife and tried to set in motion a plan that would, many decades hence, take all the camps from inside the park and place them on the perimeter. Few people could see the wisdom of his vision, but many will in the future as we seek to crowd out the last vestiges of wild lands with urban-type development.

Robbie, a person of huge integrity, was a great soldier of conservation and was prepared to stick his neck out for what he believed was right for the conservation of our wilderness, as he had done at Ngala.

Another story relating to fences began during a seminar on the restructuring of Satour – the South African Tourist Corporation – to which I was invited by Valli Moosa who was, at the time the minister of the environment and tourism in South Africa.

At the breakfast table Valli asked me: 'What do you think we should do about the elephants?'

My reply was, 'The one thing you shouldn't do is cull them. That's the old South Africa. The new South Africa is all about advancing green frontiers, putting land back under wildlife and creating space for the safari industry to thrive and provide opportunities for rural people.'

Valli told me that every single 'expert' he had spoken to told him that the elephants had to be culled. He said, 'They're destroying the biodiversity of the park. Why do you argue differently?' Valli really enjoyed a debate and I was on a roll.

'One thing you should consider is that those elephants are your stock in trade,' I replied. 'They are the way for thousands of people to be liberated from the poverty trap in which they find themselves. If you start culling them the world will shit on you. It will not work. Just drop the fence and give elephants the space and let communities and entrepreneurs build sustainable businesses based on a wildlife economy. There's plenty of talk about removing the fences between the Kruger Park and Mozambique. But nothing is happening. If you really want to understand, give me five days. I'll take you to Tanzania.'

I continued: 'What is really destroying the biodiversity of the park has nothing to do with elephants. It's about inappropriate and failed land-use practices west of the Kruger Park. That's what you should actually be looking at. I want to show you the Sand River catchment area where things have gone wrong. But I also want you to know that it's not just one river on our eastern escarpment. The same story is repeated over and over again.'

As I have said, the engagement was fierce and the debate robust but it was conducted in a good spirit.

Some months later Valli gave me those five days which we spent on the northern Tanzanian circuit.

We took the road from Ngorongoro via Olduvai Gorge to the entrance of the Serengeti where there are two stone cairns and a sign that hangs from a pole at an angle which marks the Serengeti boundary. It says, 'Held in trust for our children.' I asked the driver to stop and suggested that Valli take a photograph of the fence.

'There are no fences,' Valli replied.

'That's the first lesson,' I said. 'The second lesson is that the last 300 000 animals that we've been driving through, en route to the Serengeti, live outside the park. They don't need fences. Neither do we. Now go and take down the eastern fence of the Kruger Park.'

While we were there looking at one of the world's great open systems I suggested that we should do three things: 'Remove the eastern fence to create the Great Limpopo Transfrontier Park; ratify the Greater St Lucia Wetland Park with the inclusion of all the smaller reserves and wilderness areas right up to the Mozambique border; and form Blyde River Canyon Park which would stabilise the headwaters of the Sabi and Sand Rivers, which flow into the Kruger National Park.

'You're a politician,' I said. 'I'm a conservationist. You told me that you only deal with things that are politically deliverable. Can you deliver? Those are the three things you should do while you are in office. Can we agree?'

Valli turned to me and shook my hand. 'That's what we'll do!' And he did pretty well all he promised.

Valli Moosa's great strength was his flexibility, his ability to grasp a situation quickly and to make things happen through the political process. Soon after his return from Tanzania he called me on my cellphone from Skukuza telling me that he had two hours and wanted to look at the Sand River catchment area. This was not the normal behaviour of a minister who has his life and his diary filled for months in advance. It was exactly what I loved about him. So I mobilised a helicopter from Nelspruit, picked up Les Carlisle, picked up Valli and flew over the catchment area – all in a few hours.

When we got back he said, 'I now understand what you're talking about. I'll get Ronnie Kasrils (then minister of water affairs and forestry) on board and we'll go to work. We'll get him to donate the key catchment farms to DEAT (the department for the environment and tourism).'

Valli employed a number of talented advisers and we began the process of forming a catchment park which would protect the sources of rivers vital to the Kruger Park. A year later – with the support and cooperation of six different government departments – he declared the

Blyde River Canyon Park to be in the process of becoming a national reserve. During his tenure he also presided over the creation of both the Greater St Lucia Wetland Park and the Limpopo Transfrontier Park.

I believe that Valli was one of the most effective ministers of the environment this country will ever see and that his legacy in forming these three great parks will endure for hundreds of years and be recognised as one of Africa's great conservation achievements. Since his departure from government Valli Moosa has become president of the International Union for the Conservation of Nature (IUCN). I am sure that his contribution to conservation is not yet over.

Thabo Mbeki – the question of land ownership and land use

Two things I said to Thabo Mbeki when he visited Londolozi in the early 90s: 'During your tenure the transfrontier parks will become a reality and history will judge that they will be the greatest thing that happened on the African continent in the 21st century. The second thing is that you will have the chance to twin the pressures of land redistribution with the concept of appropriate land-use practice.'

I suggested that there was an opportunity to kill two birds with one stone: 'There's a lot of land out there that is inappropriately used. Give it to people but insist that they use it correctly.'

If I was to have a conversation with President Mbeki now I would say: 'The greatest dormant asset currently in South Africa and the one that could significantly alleviate poverty while at the same time perpetuating the maintenance and expansion of biodiversity and a conservation development model, are the former homelands. Your political structure and your new democracy have not dealt with this blight on our land. And because you haven't, economic apartheid still resides within South Africa.'

Twelve years after Thabo's visit to Londolozi, I again reminded him that nothing had been done about the homelands and how much potential there was to begin a conservation offensive in these regions. I am sure that this issue will be addressed in the near future by the government and that conservation and rural people living under a wildlife economy will be the beneficiaries.

spike milligan

9 Orme Court,
LONDON. W. 2.

3rd July, 1979

John Varty Esq.,
Londolozi Game Reserve,
26 Stanley Avenue,
Auckland Park, 2001,
Johanesburg.
South Africa.

Dear John,

I have been soliciting various people to raise money for
the Elephants.   Peter Sellers has come up with £1,500
and he would like to give the Elephant a name SATCHITANANDA.
It would be nice to give him a certificate in return, saying
he owns the Elephant, how old it is, and the name.
Money is being sent to the office in dribs and drabs from
my last television appearance, I mentioned you, and Norma
is handling it, she says she's got about £70 at the moment,
she wants to wait a week, then send it to you, she's already
been to tha bank, they will do all the necessary arrangement
Hope you are well, and everything is going O.K.

Love, light and peace,

Spike

Spike Milligan.

One person I could have learnt from in the early years was Spike Milligan. He had no place in his life for compromise and must have been the only person to turn down an invitation to the wedding of his friend Prince Charles to Diana. He told us that he declined the invitation because they planned to kill some bears so that the bear-skin busbies worn by the Queen's Guards could be remade for the wedding. The press got hold of the story. Banner headlines across England read, 'Bourgeoisie butcher bears,' says Spike Milligan. Spike, an uncompromising conservationist, passed out interviews left, right and centre, talking to all who would listen to his reason for declining the invitation to the wedding.

Spike first came to Londolozi in the 1970s. He was a great guy to take out into the bush: empathetic, sensitive and always asking difficult questions. He listened to our tale of woe – that we did not have elephants and our other wildlife was disappearing. Then he went back to England and phoned the BeeGees, Paul McCartney and Peter Sellers. He raised £1500 from each of them for elephants destined for Londolozi. The donor got to name 'his' elephant.

Spike continued his fund-raising efforts by writing to various corporations, asking for money for elephants. More often than not, he would receive long, wordy, corporate refusal letters and he would forward these to us with his comments marked in the margin, 'This is the corporate way of telling you to fuck off!' His comments were priceless and this was one of his least vulgar remarks. There was no compromise for Spike when it came to values.

We once visited him at his home in England and he told us how he nearly drowned playing school rugby. He found himself at the bottom of a loose scrum with his faced pushed into the mud and a ton of human flesh on top of him. According to him, when the scrum broke up and the game moved on, he was so deeply buried in the mud that no one could see him. When he finally recovered sufficiently to lift his head the coach shouted at him: 'Milligan, put your head down or else you'll put us all offside.' By the end of the story, which lasted for a full 20 minutes, John and I were rolling on the ground with laughter.

He was a man of enormous wit, insisting that at the end of his life, they should write on his tombstone, 'I told them I was sick.'

As one of the original Hambros investment banking team, Mark was the architect of the financial structure that got CCAfrica off the ground where, at one stage, it looked as if it would lie forever. Although our fund-raising road show across Europe and America was a tense and testing time, Mark always remained upbeat and positive with his sharp wit and wicked sense of humour and we laughed our way through days when otherwise we should have been in despair.

This conservation project, launched at the dawning of South Africa's new democracy, needed a visionary 'shepherd' investor to bring it to life. Mark and his family were just that and without his courage, foresight and vision, CCAfrica, Phinda and the opportunities created for thousands of rural people in Africa would never have happened.

It is fitting that as part of the full circle journey, Mark agreed to write the foreword to this book as he, too, has just ended a stellar chapter in his business life, having built up and now taken back into the family his own creation, Getty Images.

In the light of the growing body of information relating to global warming and declining wilderness areas, I am certain that Mark has a major role to play in advancing the cause of conservation and land restoration across our planet.

It is my fervent hope that in his lifetime he too will walk the full circle back to the original inspirations that he found in the formation of Conservation Corporation Africa and that he will continue to use his considerable influence in bringing the disciplines of business to support sustainable conservation.

Mark's brother Tara came to Phinda in the early days and did anything he could to help, including carrying luggage, welcoming guests and releasing wildlife into the new Phinda reserve. This resulted in Tara acquiring a grassroots understanding of the challenges facing the safari industry and the restoration of land under wildlife. Tara believed in our conservation ideas; he understood that we could not create islands of prosperity in a sea of poverty and that profitable conservation was the way to go into the future.

Tara has taken his involvement in Africa many steps further. He has, in his personal capacity, fully supported the Africa Foundation. In giving both his time and money he has done much to help raise education, health and other opportunities for people in the rural communities surrounding Phinda and, indeed, across Africa wherever CCAfrica operates. Furthermore, he has fully embraced the philosophy of investing in and securing land for wildlife. Using his independent resources, Tara bought land adjacent to Phinda, thereby advancing green frontiers and promoting the further expansion of the Greater St Lucia Wetland Park.

Mark and Tara are role models to future generations interested in using their influence to protect the planet from the ravages of unsustainable extraction and development.

Photograph: Richard du Toit

THE FAMILY RETURNS TO ITS ROOTS

The years after leaving CCAfrica passed quickly and before we knew where we were it was time for the family to return to its bushveld inheritance and relaunch Londolozi under a new generation of management, taking the best of the old times as well as sifting through the best we had learnt along the way. Many things had changed. In the space of 14 years, communications had advanced dramatically. In the early 1990s we had a telephone line into Londolozi that frequently broke down. One electric storm was all it took and the camps would be out of touch with the rest of the world for days. Satellite communications for the private individual were in their infancy. The personal computer was coming along but was not a household necessity. The Internet was catching on – but still slowly.

In response to what we believed would happen once the Internet took off, we converted an old tractor shed in our back garden at Londolozi into our head office and, with the advances in com-munications and Internet technology, we could reach the entire world, sending out messages on conservation to past guests and receiving information and reservations. The administration of our business turned out to be efficient and fun. No longer did we need a large office in Johannesburg to control the guest experience. Not only is this cost effective, it also offers remarkable career opportunities for those who work within the Londolozi family.

We planned that the ethos of family hospitality and the personal touch would be centre stage from the day we opened our doors to guests. We needed a person to act as the link between our experience and the exuberance of youth. Chris Kane-Berman, who was the last of the old Londolozi team prior to the signing of the 1994 CCAfrica management contract, became one of the most successful of all the managers within the CCAfrica group.

Chris cut his teeth as a cub ranger when he came to Londolozi in 1991 and he witnessed Londolozi as a family-run, well-oiled machine with a like-minded workforce and a policy of giving every member of staff the space to be the best version of themselves. He never forgot

the old Londolozi philosophies. So, when the CCAfrica management
contract was nearing its end, we were overjoyed at his decision to return
to Londolozi. He did so in the belief that his management style was
more effective in a family business than within a larger corporation.

For us Chris provided a vital ingredient as we relaunched Londolozi
onto the world market. He understood the principles of guest-focused
operations and the importance of staff training, empowerment of the
workforce and the components that were essential in the creation of
a new people-centred model in a maturing democratic South Africa.

Chris's task was also to develop new frontiers, re-benchmarking the safari experience. He is the sheet-anchor to Bronwyn and Boyd, as well as the other young men and women who are starting their careers at Londolozi. He carried with him a decade of training in the corporate environment taking care of the important disciplines required to run a smooth and efficient operation.

What had stayed the same since our early days, was that our guests came first. What we needed to do was to put energy back into our service ethic. 'Through the eyes of the guests', a mantra that had begun in the early days of Londolozi, was reinstated. All staff were asked to look at every aspect of the business as if they were seeing it for the first time. 'Moments of Truth', a concept that we had once used, was again implemented, and every manager was obliged to examine each and every aspect of the service interface. Finally the concept of 'Beyond' was introduced, inviting members of the team to look beyond what they were doing and see if more could be achieved for each of us and for themselves as individuals.

Londolozi burst onto the international stage in 2007 with Shan and Bronwyn leading the marketing charge. Chris Kane-Berman steadied the operational ship, ensuring delivery of the product. Boyd came on board to head up our land care programme, managing the entire estate, which required continual observation to ensure that we generated maximum energy flow from the land. Boyd also monitors the field operations enjoying a strong rapport with our 32 senior trackers and rangers, who bring a wealth of experience to the game drive experience.

The new shift in direction at Londolozi begins with finding the relationship between the health of the human spirit and the health of the last vestiges of the wilderness. What we perceive as important is to reduce man's footprint on the land and focus more on the richness of the meditative experience in the African bushveld. The objective is to lead the Londolozi team of rangers into uncharted frontiers of wilderness learning. On the list of significant changes from the old days is that Londolozi is now part of the six million acre transfrontier park which includes the Kruger Park and the Sabi Sand Game Reserve and spreads further east into Mozambique. We hope to see the park spread west to include the headwaters of the rivers which feed our biodiversity. With the recognition of the Blyde River Reserve and more space for wildlife, this plan has become far more of a possibility and when it is eventually recognised, it will again result in the linking up of nature's ecological plan, mountain to sea, high rainfall to low rainfall, from forests to grasslands and to sparse bushveld, ensuring that migratory animals such as wildebeest, elephants and buffalo will continually pass through our lands.

Another key change is that we now straddle the Sand River with the old Sparta farm to the south-west and the new Marthly farm to the north-east. The two farms share a common boundary but offer a wonderful improvement in the diversity of landscape. Marthly is wild and beautiful and includes many spectacular rocky outcrops and high vantage points from which to survey the wilderness stretching out before us. The Manyeleti River winds its way through the centre of the Marthly property adding significantly to the leopard habitat of the greater Londolozi area.

We changed the camp configurations and created smaller, exclusive camps with individual teams tasked with running them. The result is that the layers of hotel management that appeared during our absence have been replaced by a warm intimate atmosphere in which a host or hostess cares for our guests. Each of the five camps has a theme. The Varty Camp is where the fire is lit each evening in the same spot chosen by my grandfather more than 80 years ago. The original four rondavels where the family lived and where my grandmother shooed a lioness away with a kitchen towel (mistaking the lion for a dog), are now used to show John's conservation films or for Internet connections, as a library containing early books of the bushveld and to house memorabilia of the past. Pioneer Camp is steeped in the early history of Londolozi. The Camp recalls names such as Charles Boyd Varty, Winnis Mathebula and Frank Unger, the original pioneers of what has now become Londolozi. Founders Camp honours guides who, over the past three and a half decades, worked at Londolozi and contributed to its building. Then there are two other top of the range small camps: Tree Camp with its emphasis on elegance and simplicity, which has six private suites; and the magical Granite Camp, with three suites looking over the granite outcrops of the Sand River. They are among the most exclusive, stylish and luxurious camps in Africa.

Supporting these camps, which are linked by a pathway along the bank of the Sand River, is the Londolozi Life Centre and cardiovascular gym. This facility goes beyond a traditional spa and offers therapies designed to help our guests create a balance – in body, mind and soul – and take away some of the stress of modern living. The therapies harmonise with the rhythms and cycles of nature and are designed to capture the very essence of healthy living.

The Londolozi staff village has been completely revitalised and is now hosting guests. This Shangaan village gives a glimpse into a rich culture of the past. The Londolozi Learning Centre at the village is addressing the educational needs of each individual who works within our community.

Photograph: Elsa Young

| *The heart and soul of Londolozi*

Last spring was one of sheer magic. The rains came early and within a week the bushveld was painted with fresh shades of green. Thousands of impala dropped their young and there were baby rhino, gangly giraffe, hippos born in the shallows of the river, kudu, waterbuck and wildebeest calves and litters of fat warthog piglets. Of course, with all the prey species thriving, so did the predators. Prides of lion, hyena and leopard flourished and even wild dogs, which we had not seen for a while, turned up at Londolozi. Few elephants live permanently in one place but the Kruger elephants seem to have rediscovered the treasure trove across the Sand River and we now have a never-ending procession of herds passing by.

On top of that, we have the most exciting viewing of leopards that you could find anywhere in Africa. Twenty-five years ago Ken Tinley told us, 'Look after the land and the animals will look after themselves.' We followed his advice and soon after that we had our first leopard sighting in decades. Today we have research to prove that land management is directly correlated to the productivity of wildlife. Because of the work done 30 years ago, we and our guests are privileged to watch leopards on the hunt, leopard mothers caring and teaching their cubs and the unbelievable linking of leopard families together.

Lastly, we have a new generation of management. The old and experienced are introducing the young and vibrant. What a formidable combination. Bronwyn, stylish and dynamic, represents the new face of Londolozi to the marketplace. Boyd, charismatic and experienced, is introducing wilderness healing into the safari experience. They are backed by Allan Taylor and John Varty who will play the role of senior elders in taking Londolozi forward.

At the time of writing we are all considering the vexed subject of land ownership and transformation. Together, in collective debate within our community, we are facing the macro challenges of transient politics, maintenance of biodiversity, river restoration and individual endeavour towards right relations between each other and with the earth in the ever-changing Africa.

THE FULL CIRCLE

When I sit on my balcony overlooking the Sand River and look back over the past 35 years, I wonder how I survived. If we had been cats, I think the whole family would – long ago – have used up all nine of their lives!

I recall all the close shaves we had with Africa's high mountains, strong rivers, fearless tribes, violent storms and fearsome predators. I am reminded of the woolly-necked stork that shattered the windshield of the Cessna 402 on our final approach into Richards Bay, knocking out the pilot and leaving Shan and the other passengers, including myself, sitting in a pilotless plane, covered in glass, feathers and blood. I reflect on the occasion at Londolozi when I watched a black mamba, one of Africa's most lethal snakes, slither over my 11-year-old son's leg. I could only watch and pray that he would not move a muscle. I remember the formidable look on the Maasai headman's face when he told me: 'Dar es Salaam does not speak for this land. The Maasai are in charge here.' And the day I walked out of the front door of my home at Londolozi into a pride of lions and for a moment felt like Daniel in the lions' den.

I remember the calls that can come at any time of the day or night, 365 days of the year, the one that all safari operators dread – 'There's been an accident.' A guest has been killed by a lion. Violent storm: the camp's underwater. Staff member hit by a buffalo: airlifted out of the Serengeti at 2am. Cameraman killed by elephant. Land Rover rolls. Guest paralysed. Lightning strike: two girls survive, both have broken pelvises. Another lightning strike: Pioneer Camp lounge burnt down – insurance company informed. Aircraft hits trees: no injuries. Ranger kills buffalo on top of guest: one person injured but stable. Guest falls over log: splits shin – seventy-five stitches. Bandits hit camp – staff tied up and $10 000 missing. Giraffe trips over Land Rover: guest concussed.

Suicides, accidents, injuries that require immediate attention, accidental discharge of guns, vehicles flipped – the safari business is not for the faint-hearted.

And then I recall the mistake I nearly made trading family values for business pressure and

1926 to present - the circle is complete

how, thankfully, we reconnected with our precious son and daughter and together relaunched Londolozi. Not least of all, in completing this circle of our lives, we move forward with a wider experience and a greater understanding of the world around us, grateful for all the experiences and lessons we have been given.

And what of the many other positive things? What of the Londolozi model that brought our bushveld farm back to life? Of Nelson Mandela and his great understanding of our story? What of the thousands of people with jobs in the safari industry across Africa? What of Phinda, developed from an unknown entity to become internationally known? And what of the dream of the Greater St Lucia Wetland Park and other transfrontier parks and conservancies with no fences? What of the explosion of private land and gameland under wildlife since the establishment of Phinda? And what of the indisputable fact that the arid regions of Africa best serve her rural people under wildlife? What of the truly sustainable careers that have been created in five countries in Africa? And what a joy to think how the ideas of a few crazy entrepreneurs have impacted on the lives of so many people. And how the safari industry has grown in southern Africa. Yes, indeed, in South Africa tourism surpassed gold as a foreign revenue earner in 2006. This has been a rollercoaster ride of epic proportions.

Along our journey we met many interesting people and learnt some hard but wonderful lessons. We were exposed both to the rich and famous and to the beautiful warmth and energy of Africa's rural people. We learnt how corporate finance works and the different strengths of large corporations when compared with family businesses. Notwithstanding all the problems we faced, we hope that we left a positive trail behind us.

In 1972 we started a 20-year rearguard action to defend our land from expropriation by the apartheid regime. This battle spawned the concept of the economic viability of wildlife and the Londolozi model. By the 1990s that model was mature, defined, successful and ready to be used in a new democratic South Africa to promote the concept of the economics of land under wildlife.

For the next 10 years, taking all we had learnt at Londolozi as the springboard, we exported the model in various shapes and forms to different parts of sub-Saharan Africa. By the turn of the century it showed us a diversity of landscapes and of people unparalleled anywhere in the world and it showed us a continent that has done the best job of all in preserving and advancing nature's great master plan.

With the family back at Londolozi and the closing of the circle of our journey, fundamental to everything that we do in the future will be respect for the sanctity and the wildness of the land.

Every drop of water that we pump into or away from our camps, every bag of waste that has to be disposed of, every plane that flies overhead, the tracks that we make, the vehicles that are driven across the wilderness – in fact every imprint that man leaves behind – will be analysed with great care against a backdrop – of respect for the sanctity of a wild area. We are aware that if we want to leave this land to posterity as we found it, we will have to redefine the multi-use economic viability model upon which Londolozi was founded.

My belief is that when we do so, far from reducing the overall safari experience for our guests, we will add another dimension. We will make guests feel more involved and their wildlife experience will be enhanced by a feeling of being closer to nature. I'm sure it will be more wild and more exciting. The experience will be driven less by what you consume and more by what you feel. Most of all, we want to keep in focus our original vision which is embodied in our original mission statement written soon after we discovered the Zulu word: Londolozi: 'The protector of all living things'.

As we put our 21st century ideas into practice, we can relax for a brief moment. Our home fires are burning brighter than ever before. We have invested wisely by expanding our land across the Sand River with the result that Londolozi's game viewing is better than it has ever been in my lifetime. In the summer of 2007/2008, the land could not have been more stunning: the rivers and streams ran clear, the trees were a tapestry of every conceivable shade of green, and every living thing – from the elephants to the leopards, the giraffe and the rhinoceros – was flourishing. Even the birds seemed brighter and their songs louder. I may have to concede that here my imagination may have come into play – or perhaps it is because it is such a contrast to the dreary world of boardrooms and courtrooms that we left behind. Most significantly, we have come out of the last 17 years on our feet, somewhat wiser and with absolute clarity of who we are and what we stand for. In the words of our great teacher, Ken Tinley: 'We had returned to our own fire. It was the one that always kept us warm.'

The five lodges on the Sand River are luxurious, beautifully appointed, filled with soul, with history, with love and care. In October 2006, 80 years after our grandfather first lit the fire at his camp on the banks of the Sand River, we arranged a special Full Circle Reunion for all our old friends who walked the road with us and supported our dream. We owed them a vote of gratitude. We welcomed their children back to the fireside at Londolozi where they had spent so many of their years. The Londolozi 'alumni', otherwise known as the Old Boys/Girls Club which consists of anyone that has ever worked for Londolozi, was officially inaugurated on 6 October 2006 in White River, Mpumalanga, and it is our hope that, in the future, it may call many young warriors to join the battle for the earth to return to a sustainable symmetry.

And what of Dave Varty?

On the surface of things he's accident-prone. He's a wild card. He's scatterbrained. He can't see any reason for seriously rich people to want to get richer. But let's go back and examine how loose the cannon really is.

Londolozi is working. CCAfrica, supported by some of the world's most wealthy families, is a phenomenon across Africa, Asia and South America. It has survived a tough 'growing-up' period and hopefully with maturity, will find its way back to its original philosophy of being a leader in conservation offensives all over the world. The Serengeti of the South, which straddles the Orange/Gariep River, is being born. Corridors for elephants: perhaps? Fences? Many are gone. The Blyde River Catchment Park is a reality while the Greater St Lucia Wetland Park has been proclaimed a World Heritage Site and one day Phinda will be part of the Maputaland transfrontier conservation offensive linking Greater St Lucia Park to Tembe, Kosi Bay and Reserva d'Elefantas d'Maputa in Mozambique.

In the wheel of life my job was always to see the way ahead, pioneer it, shift existing paradigms, inspire the team and then move on. The plan I worked to and the results – despite all the ups and downs – are there to be seen.

And what of the future and the lessons learnt?

To the outside world, when you appear to have been 'successful', the opposite is often the case. The perceived setbacks are the times of true growth and learning. These are the times when you discover that much of 'success' as well as much of 'failure' is an illusion.

We have created a small space at Londolozi called Sanctum. It is intended to be a place for people to come to when society or illness has delivered a setback in their lives. It is a place where you can sit quietly, find perspective and continue to find respite from the trials you have been through. In the future we hope that people will come who have been hit by the passage of life – whether it is cancer, the so-called golden handshake that destroys so many men and women, whether it is relationships that have broken down or loves lost. Whatever it may be, they will be welcome to sit here and watch nature as it passes by. Those elephants will help heal their wounds. As will this tree and this wind that shakes the leaves and bends the grass. And these leopard orchids. Nature at peace has an extraordinary impact on the human spirit.

We've come to understand that this great intelligent being around us that we call the wilderness is a healer. People don't analyse why they like to go to the bush. I believe the reason is that when you place yourself close to nature, it pours balm on your troubles. It calms and makes you feel good.

Ian Player said that in the future, the wilderness will become a necessity, even if we only stand on the edge and stare into it.

Recently, psychologist Dr Ian MacCullam said that we visit the wilderness because we are homesick. Most of all I believe that everyone has a deep need to be reconnected to this land – call it our 13th DNA. You cannot watch a leopard mother teaching and caring for its cubs without feeling your spirit lifted by the natural beauty of this world. Alongside this, all else is insignificant.

I would like to see Londolozi become the change it wishes to see – a microcosm of a South Africa filled with hope, friendship and a willingness to coexist; a place where the full energy flows of the land are unlocked and where the individual spirit and the capacities of Africa's people will become evident. In the next few years I will bring influential people to Londolozi and let them experience the warmth, theatre and energy of Africa and I will invite them to participate.

The rest of my life will be about making a 'significant' contribution: to
serve, to teach, and, yes, to rally, cajole and negotiate for more space for
the wild creatures with whom we share this planet.

By the turn of the century the economics of the Londolozi model and the safari industry in general, had become a real contributor to the economies of the various sub-Saharan countries. But a new enemy is emerging – the so-called tourism double-edged sword. This is a situation that develops when the very resource which attracts visitors is overrun, and even destroyed, by the impact of too many visitors.

The Florida Everglades, Everest and the Himalayas, the Great Barrier Reef, Kilimanjaro, the French Riviera, the Algarve, Ngorongoro Crater, the antiquities of Egypt and Uluru are examples of where this problem is already evident. Too many people visiting an exciting safari destination, beyond its tourism-carrying capacity, sow the seed of its demise.

The natural progression for opening up a wildlife area follows a certain procedure. First the area is discovered by pioneer operators who begin a simple, limited operation. It becomes popular and the operation grows. Accommodation is improved to refine the guest experience and meet consumer needs. Soon the essence of the wild area, which was the original attraction, begins to be overrun by man-made artifacts, camps, and lodges and their related consequences. Only after the architects, designers and development teams have moved on are the operators left with the task of running the lodge from day to day. With this responsibility comes the maintenance staff, the electricians, plumbers, fridge mechanics etc. All necessary to keep the 'tourism' infrastructure working. It's expensive and it adds to the load of people entering the reserve over the tracks to these remote camps.

When planning a development of any sort, in a remote wilderness area, it is important to remember that developing the lodge or camp is like having sex but operating it is like having a baby. Once created it brings a lifetime of commitment and ongoing impacts into the region

While spreadsheets and business plans dictate more beds and more tours to make more money, the sustainability of fragile ecosystems is a factor that cannot be ignored. Can the Ngorongoro Crater cope with 350 vehicles a day? What is the carrying capacity of visitors to any one park? Human density, vehicles, aircraft, noise pollution and too many electric lights are some of the new challenges we face as we invade the last strongholds of the wilderness with our safari models and our western 'for-profit' consumer approach.

What may be considered by conservation purists to be an overdone development will be seen in a completely different way by the urban traveller who has just arrived from New York, Hong Kong or São Paulo, and yet again by a property developer who is used to filling small plots of land with high-density condominiums. There are no finite measures. But to me, what is clear is that over the next 10 years, as the industry grows, the management challenges will not be about elephants or poaching, but about the creeping impact of tourism development that will threaten the last vestiges of a pristine wilderness.

On the positive side, this same growth and success of the safari industry could and should be used as an advocacy for advancing an outward creative conservation offensive in Africa. Let's use this success to create new wildernesses, more transfrontier parks, more conservancies and corridors transforming land under failed agricultural projects and faulty political ideologies back to wildlife.

Our first step began at Londolozi in the 1970s when we were threatened with expropriation. We were able to demonstrate the economic viability of land under wildlife and the importance of drawing people into sharing the benefits.

When I first visited the Phinda farmlands, all the derelict relics of failed agriculture were there to see – the broken fences, the rusted machinery, the sisal gone wild. And, of course, the surrounding communities living in abject poverty with no prospects of earning a living. Today, what joy it is to see Phinda vibrant with wildlife, the free-ranging black and white rhinos, elephants, buffalo, lions, leopards and, indeed, some of the best cheetah viewing on the African continent. In a little over a decade the communities surrounding Phinda have changed dramatically: People are earning a living, children are attending schools, the regional economy is vibrant and careers are sustainable.

Countless similar examples exist across Africa of rebuilding ecosystems and regional economies on the success of wildlife-based economy.

Mozambique recently set aside 43 000 square kilometres of land as wildlife concessions. And Gorongosa is being restored. Is it possible that this enlightened African leadership, spurred on by the obvious potential of the safari industry will use their influence to connect the Selous Game Reserve in Tanzania via the Niassa Corridor, to these newly formed concessions and onward via Lake Malawi, Gorongoza, Zinave and Bahine National Parks connecting to the Great Limpopo Transfrontier Park?

Is it not an impossible dream that this corridor of wildlife could continue westward to the Blyde River Canyon and onwards via Loskop Dam Nature Reserve to the Cradle of Humankind linking to the proposed corridor between Pilanesberg Game Reserve and Madikwe Game Reserve, Kalahari Transfrontier westwards, northwards and beyond? Add to this the vision for the creation of the 'Serengeti of the South', reinstating the springbok migrations in the southern Free State and Northern Cape – and we could have one single corridor of wildlife from Selous to the Cape.

Is it a pipe dream or a reality? Time will tell.

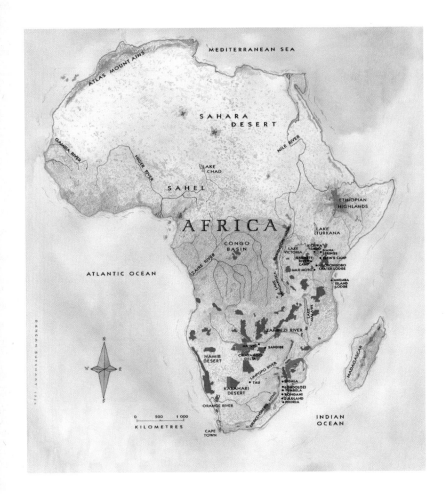

The remnant parks of Africa

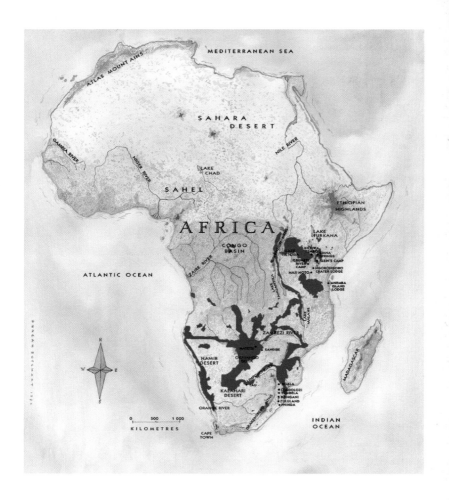

Corridors of wildlife - Africa, the adventure destination of the world.
Is it a pipe dream or a reality? Time will tell.

Anderson, Ray. *Mid-Course Correction: toward a sustainable enterprise: the interface model*. Peregrinzilla Press, 1999.

Bard, Alexander and Jan Söderqvist. *Netocracy*. Reuters/Pearsall UK, 2002.

Barnhill, David Landis and Roger S Gottlieb (eds). *Deep Ecology and World Religions: new essays on sacred ground*. Albany: State University of New York Press, 2001.

Benyus, Janine M. *Biomimicry: innovation inspired by nature*. Harper Perennial, 2002.

Berry, T. *The Great Work: our way into the future*. New York: Bell Tower, 1999.

Collins, Jim. *Good to Great*. Random House Business Books, 2001.

Devall, Bill and George Sessions. *Deep Ecology – living as if nature mattered*. Gibbs M Smith Inc, 1985.

Elkington, John. *Cannibals With Forks: the triple bottom line of the 21st century*. Capstone, 1997.

Frankel, Carl. *In Earth's Company: business, environment, and the challenge of sustainability*. New Society Publishers, 1998.

Hartmann, Thom. *The Last Hours of Ancient Sunlight: waking up to personal and global transformation.* London: Hodder & Stoughton, 2001.

Hart, Stuart. *Capitalism at the Crossroads: the unlimited business opportunities in solving the world's most difficult problems*. Upper Saddle River, N J, 2005.

Hawken, Paul. *Ecology of Commerce: a declaration of sustainability*. Harper-Collins, 1993.

Hawken, Paul, Amory B Lovins and L Hunter Lovins. *Natural Capitalism: creating the next Industrial Revolution*. Little Brown, 1999.

Hubbard, Barbara Marx. *Conscious Evolution: awakening our social potential*. New World Library, 1998.

McDonough, William and Michael Braungart. *Cradle to Cradle: remaking the way we make things*. Farrar, Straus & Giroux, 2002.

Nattrass, Brian F and Mary E Altomare. *The Natural Step for Business: wealth, ecology and the evolutionary corporation*. Gabriola Island, BC: New Society, 1999.

Quinn, Daniel. *Beyond Civilisation: humanity's next great adventure.* Random House, 2000.

Redfield, James. *The Celestine Prophecy.* Grand Central Publishing, 1995.

Schmidheiny, Stephan and Federico J L Zorraquin. *Financing Change: the financial community, eco-efficiency, and sustainable development.* Cambridge, MA: The MIT Press, 1996.

Sessions, George. *Deep Ecology for the Twenty-First Century.* Boston: Libri, 1995.

Stone, Joshua. *The Hidden Mysteries: ETs, ancient mystery schools and ascension.* Light Technology Publishing, 1996.

Toffler, Alvin. *The Third Wave.* Bantam Books, 1980.

http://www.pegasuscom.com/